TEACHING CHILDREN
HOW TO PRAY AND THE REASONS FOR IT

Guiding Parents and Grandparents in Teaching Children the Power of Prayer

Vernon J. DeFlanders

Table Of Content

INTRODUCTION

As a believing parent, grandparent, or other caregiver, you already know the power of prayer and how to pray in faith and trust. Facing life's many challenges leads you to a deep, intuitive knowledge of when it is time to use prayer to nourish your spirit, give praise and thanks, or ask for help and guidance. For children, it might be difficult to understand why prayer is needed; after all, they have only basic needs, and their parents usually fulfill these. In this book, we'll explore strategies and tools to introduce children to prayer and help them understand the how, when, and why of effective and uplifting prayer. We'll also discover how prayer adds to a child's spiritual growth and emotional well-being and address some common questions and challenges children may have in their journey toward a deeper understanding of God and a more connected faith.

It is never too early to start bringing prayer into a child's life. Caregiving also includes spiritual care; therefore, we can help build our children's spiritual foundation to give them a solid base from which they can grow ever closer to God throughout their lives.

We start by looking into the importance and basics of prayer and its role in fostering children's spirituality and faith. Chapter 1 dives into the foundation of prayer. We'll explore the beauty and meaning of prayer and how it fits into children's understanding of spirituality. In teaching children how to pray, it is imperative that they have a concept of sincerity and understand that sincere prayer will connect them to an unseen yet omnipresent God. There is a section dedicated to the types of prayer and how to guide children toward silent and verbal prayers, as well as how to bring physical expressions such as folding hands into their prayers as a means of focus. Then, we'll discuss why prayer matters to children and why it is spiritually beneficial to start praying early in life.

In Chapter 2, we'll explore how to create a prayerful atmosphere. Having a special place set apart for prayer instills a sense of the sacred and holy. With a special prayer place that a child can enjoy and look forward to using, we move on to ideas on how to make prayer part of a child's daily routine through morning and bedtime rituals, visual aids, symbols, and interactive tools such as prayer beads and prayer diaries. We end the chapter with methods to make prayer a family activity that will strengthen bonds not only with God but also with each other.

Chapter 3 is all about practical tips for teaching children how to pray. We look at age-appropriate language and explanations and how to introduce various types of prayer, such as traditional and spontaneous prayer. We also explore how to help children use their natural creativity in their spiritual development.

Praying at various set times during the day helps bring prayer into a child's daily routine. In Chapter 4, we discuss how prayer time can foster gratitude, appreciation, and strong family bonds. Morning, mealtime, bedtime, and special occasions enable children to make a spiritual connection with their daily experiences. This can be a great source of strength, comfort, and joy.

In Chapter 5, we delve into the impact of prayer on a child's emotional well-being. Children can experience stress, fears, and anxiety, and prayer can be a trusted source of strength during difficult times. Learning in childhood how to turn to prayer to cope with daily stress lays the foundation for a resilient, confident, and positive adulthood.

Bible stories are featured in Chapter 6, where we focus on stories that demonstrate the power of prayer and how to incorporate these stories into children's prayer time. We'll also see how discussing Bible stories can inspire children not only in prayer but also in making choices that align with biblical values.

Fun is the main theme of Chapter 7, where we discuss the use of arts and crafts to get children excited about prayer and help them express their spiritual life. From decorating prayer journals and making a prayer request log to playing prayer-themed games, painting Bible scenes, performing skits, and creating prayer bracelets, children learn to link creativity to a prayerful connection with their Creator.

After the fun of Chapter 7, we turn to difficult questions in Chapter 8. Sometimes, prayers don't get answered the way we expect or go unanswered, which can be confusing for a child. We discuss some of the more common questions regarding prayer and how to answer them in a way that encourages spiritual resilience and trust in God's higher plan. The chapter includes strategies to help children understand and cope with the disappointment of unanswered prayers and address their doubts while balancing faith and logic.

Chapter 9 explores the prayer customs of other religions and the personal stories of faith from their own community. This broadens a child's knowledge of various cultures and fosters a sense of belonging to their own spiritual heritage. We explore how being rooted in a solid faith tradition provides a deep spiritual connection not only to God but also to other believers.

Prayer isn't something only for emergencies; it is an integral part of spiritual development and, as such, should be done consistently. Just like physical exercise or studying, it takes dedication and persistence to bear good fruit. In Chapter 10, we focus on practical tools to keep up a consistent prayer habit. We look at goal setting and help children define their expectations of prayer, as well as encourage them to look at their own past prayers. They'll be surprised at how many were answered in ways they didn't notice!

In Chapter 11, we discuss the expansion of prayer from a solo activity to a prayer group. In a prayer group, children learn how to work as a team with others who share the same values. This gives children the opportunity to develop empathy and selflessness. It also provides children with a spiritual community where they can have a sense of belonging while learning to consider the needs of others.

We end our prayer journey with a celebration of prayer achievements. In Chapter 12, we encourage children to celebrate the development of their spirituality by looking at how prayer has guided their behavior and mindset. Celebrating prayer provides a child with insight into their own relationship with God and other people. It encourages them to continue in faithful prayer with joy and gratitude.

Chapter 1

THE FOUNDATION OF PRAYER

Let's explore exactly what prayer is and how it fits into children's spiritual lives. We'll look into prayer from a child's perspective, how prayer nourishes spiritual growth, different types of prayer, and the benefits of starting an active prayer life as early as possible.]

What Is Prayer?

When we pray, we communicate with the divine. To truly connect with a power so much greater than ourselves, we need to approach prayer with a humble spirit and show respect by focusing on our words. Prayer from the heart means more than elaborate speeches without sincerity, and we realize through the dialogue of prayer that we are dependent upon God for guidance and forgiveness.

Prayer can be spur-of-the-moment or part of a ritual, such as bedtime Bible time or a church service. It doesn't matter at what time we pray, but having prayer as part of a spiritual routine helps us grow a deeper connection with God. God is always ready to listen to His children, always ready to ease our fears and comfort our tears, and always has a greater plan to have all events in our lives work for our own good. All we have to do is talk to Him! That's what prayer boils down to: talking to God.

Where is God?

When we pray, children may wonder why we speak to someone who isn't there. They don't see God, so they might think God is the same as an imaginary friend or that God is make-believe. It is important to explain to children that God doesn't have a body like we do, which only has one set of ears to listen to prayers. God can do anything and listen to everyone on Earth simultaneously because He isn't limited to human hearing.

The Intention of Prayer

Suppose we simply tell children that prayer is asking God to do things for us or give us what we want. In that case, children are likely to interpret God as a means of wish fulfillment and prayer, akin to shopping at a candy store with indulgent parents. Make it clear to children that prayer is talking to God about their feelings, things they are grateful for, and their fears and worries. They also need to understand that God might answer prayers in ways we don't always understand.

Even adults sometimes find it difficult to stay focused during prayer and avoid being distracted by trivial thoughts. Children can maintain their focused intention during prayer, but usually not for long periods. Short or spontaneous prayers are more suitable for children. Help your children stay focused by minimizing distractions at prayer time, such as switching off the TV or radio.

Connection to Faith

Prayer can strengthen a child's connection to faith and values in several ways. Let's take a look at some of them:

- Prayer helps develop a child's self-awareness and introspection. By evaluating their needs and those of others in preparation for prayer, a child becomes more mindful of how they affect the world around them. This not only guides them to act according to the values of their faith but also helps them grow toward a mature mindset.

- When a child has the opportunity to participate in community or family prayer, it makes them feel connected not only to their faith but also to others who share their faith and values. This can be a great comfort and a source of spiritual and moral guidance.

- The Gospels tell us that God has a special place in His heart for children. Children who approach God through prayer connect with Him from a point of view of innocence and trust that we find difficult as adults. This allows children to form a deep and natural connection with the divine.

- As children start to navigate the world and broaden their community through schoolmates and friends, they discover their unique identity and how they fit in with peers. Prayer offers them the ability to strengthen their sense of identity by letting them know that, at their core, they are children of God and part of a community of believers. Having a strong sense of belonging and personal identity can give children the confidence to resist peer pressure.

- Prayer rituals, such as family prayer in the mornings or communal prayer at church, reinforce social bonds and make children feel safe and connected to something greater than themselves.

- Being able to connect to God through prayer gives children the advantage of resilience. Through faith, children can cope with many hardships and challenges without turning to unhealthy coping mechanisms such as alcohol and violent outbursts.

- In a world where money is essential for survival, education, and more, it is easy to become ungrateful and selfish. By regularly expressing sincere gratitude in prayer, children learn the difference between value and price and how to appreciate their blessings.

All in all, prayer is essential for spiritual growth, and children can greatly benefit from the connection, comfort, and guidance that a connection with God offers.

The Different Types of Prayer

There are three types of prayer that are suitable for children. Let's explore these types and discuss ideas for making them part of your child's spiritual routine.

Verbal Prayer

Verbal prayers involve praying out loud. This method is probably the easiest for children who get distracted easily or find it hard to pray silently. Verbal prayers can be spontaneous or memorized. Young children often find memorized prayers easier and can learn them quickly if they are simple and short. Here are some everyday prayers you can teach your child to pray out loud during prayer time, keeping in mind that it is okay for a child to forget some of the words:

- "Dear God, thank you for today. I love you. Amen" (Suitable for toddlers of age 1–3).

- "Dear God, thank you for blessing me and watching over me. Thank you for my family, home, food, and toys. I pray in Jesus's name. Amen" (Ages 4–6).

- "Dear God, thank you for your blessings and guidance. Please walk beside me and help me be kind, honest, and good. Bless my family, teachers, and friends. I pray in Jesus' name. Amen" (Ages 7–12).

Prayers can become longer and more detailed as the child gets older.

Children older than 12 can recite the *Lord's Prayer*, compose their own prayer to memorize, or pray spontaneously to praise God, express their gratitude, and ask for His help and blessings.

It takes time to learn anything new, so don't give up if your children can't remember all the words. Here are some methods you can try to make the learning process easier:

- Use gestures to emphasize the words. For example, when saying "Thy kingdom come," you can hold your hands in a circle above your head to signify a crown.

- Oftentimes, it is much easier to remember a song than a text. Singing the *Lord's Prayer*, or if you have a tin ear, clapping your hands to create a rhythm for the words, can be a fun way to learn!

- Much of learning is built on simple, old-fashioned repetition. Teach a prayer a few words at a time, and let your children repeat it several times after you. To make it easier to remember, add some fun by using different voices. God created us with a sense of humor, and He knows that the young ones learn best when they enjoy the process. I believe that God smiles with loving, Fatherly amusement when we teach our children!

Silent Prayer

By saying the words only in their heads, children can talk to God about private issues they would be embarrassed about if they had to vocalize them in front of family or a prayer group. Silent prayer provides a safe space to seek divine guidance without fear of being called out or judged.

Very young children, or children who have abandonment issues, may associate silence with absence. They might not understand or be uncomfortable with the idea of communicating without sound. Their experiences have taught them that it is necessary to speak to be heard, and speaking in one's head is talking only to themselves.

Children can start silent prayer around the age of five or six—generally when they are old enough to start questioning existence and God. Once they begin to wonder about the nature of God, they are ready to understand the concept of silent prayer that reaches God through trust and faith. Never force children to pray verbally or silently, as this is counterproductive and not in the spirit of love. If children are forced, they will end up feeling resentment and frustration and will consider prayer as a burden best avoided.

Silent prayer can include things such as imagining being at a biblical event to seek guidance, evaluating the day to see where we strayed from our faith and values, praising God or expressing gratitude mentally, revisiting hurtful memories and asking God for healing and forgiveness, and sitting quietly while talking to God in our minds as if we are composing a letter to a dear and trusted friend. Children are capable of all of these ways of silent prayer, and they can probably think of more! The key is to take a few moments to be still, trust that God is listening without having to hear the words, and communicate from the heart.

Here are some tips on how to teach children to start praying silently:

1. Put all distractions away and turn off devices. This can be made into a fun game where the child has to find anything that can lead their thoughts away from prayer, such as a phone, TV, magazines, or a favorite toy.

2. Then, show your child how to breathe slowly and deeply to become calm and ready to speak to God.

3. Most children focus better on silent prayer when their eyes are closed. They still need to turn off devices and put distractions away; otherwise, they might be tempted to "peek" and lose their focus. You can close your eyes and ask the child to close theirs too.

4. Then, tell your child that you're going to talk to God in your head to tell Him about your day and ask for His help, blessings, and advice. Encourage your child to do the same for a minute or two.

5. After the short day-sharing prayer, praise and worship God out loud, and tell your child that they can end their silent prayer with silent praise and worship.

6. Answer any questions your child might have about how to pray silently. Keep in mind that there isn't a right or wrong way to pray silently. The goal of silent prayer is to talk to God privately.

7. Give the child time to sit undisturbed in their room or let them go for a walk alone in a garden or some other quiet place to pray silently by themselves.

8. Encourage regular silent prayer to help them build a personal relationship with God.

In the next chapter, we'll discuss prayer routines, including morning and evening prayers, as well as prayers for saying grace.

Physical Expressions as Part of Prayer

Children naturally use their bodies to express themselves. They jump at the chance to tell stories using mimicry and gestures, love to leap and run, and enjoy twirling around to see the world spinning by. Movement is part of the way they explore and interact with their environment, and it can be used to enhance their experience of prayer.

Movements particular to prayer use the body to mark prayer time as special and sacred. It is for this reason that we close our eyes, kneel, fold our hands, or lift our hands heavenward. These physical expressions help us focus on only our communication with God.

Bringing physicality into prayer is more than merely holding our hands and legs in a particular manner. God is pleased when we put all of our being into His worship. Our bodies are His temple, and a temple is an ideal place for prayer. Therefore, it is fine to sing our prayers, kneel in humility or stand in awe, bow our heads or lift them upward, and wave our hands or fold them together. Even those with physical disabilities are still temples of God, and His presence is within all believers.

Our body language during worship and prayer can affect other people. For example, if you walk into a prayer group or church service and people are mumbling along with the hymns or sitting stiffly with absent-minded expressions during prayer, will you believe that the Spirit is present? Approach worship, praise, and prayer as a Spirit-filled temple, and the joy of being with God will comfort, support, and inspire others as well.

The only thing God asks of us regarding prayer is to be sincere and to pray to communicate with Him, not to impress others. When teaching your child to pray, let them use their bodies in ways they are comfortable with during private prayer. However, in a prayer group, family prayer circle, or church, they shouldn't use their bodies in a way that can be distracting to others. For instance, dancing and waving their arms while shouting praises are fine in their rooms but out of place elsewhere, except for congregations or groups where physical expression during prayer is accepted and encouraged.

Why Prayer Matters to Children

We know why prayer matters to us; it is a connection with our Heavenly Father whereby we can share our concerns and joys, worship and praise, and ask for help and guidance. Prayer means even more to children as they are still developing. The benefits of prayer during childhood pave the way for lifelong spirituality and faith. Let's delve a little deeper into why prayer matters to children.

Emotional Well-Being

Prayer allows children to connect with God, which gives them a sense of purpose. Life isn't meaningless when you have a personal relationship with the Creator of all life!

Being part of a prayer group or other spiritual community gives a child a sense of belonging. The child can find support and encouragement in the group, which combats feelings of loneliness. This support is especially valuable for shy children who don't make friends easily.

Even scientists have to agree that prayer has uplifting effects on emotional well-being. A study found that regular prayer is linked to more positive emotional processing and expression, as well as a higher sense of purpose and forgiveness in adolescents and young adults (Chen & VanderWeele, 2018).

Another scientific study has shown that people who pray often have a lower incidence of depression and anxiety and are more likely to be optimistic (Anderson & Nunnelley, 2016).

Spiritual Growth

Praying for others teaches children to be considerate of the needs and circumstances of others. Children begin to realize and understand that there are people who seem happy or healthy on the outside but are depressed, in mourning, lonely, ill, worried, or financially struggling. Praying for others fosters empathy, understanding, and the ability to see beyond the surface.

When praying for someone else who is having difficulties, children learn to be grateful for their own blessings. They see that others face struggles that they don't have to endure, which makes them more aware of the many ways their own lives are blessed.

Relationship Building

By building a relationship with the Father through prayer, a child lays the foundation for connecting with all of the Father's creations. Recognizing that both animals and people are beings originating from the same source enables a child to develop relationships that are kind and respectful.

Children who formulate their own prayers and do not always rely on memorized prayer learn how to express their needs, worries, deep thoughts, and emotions. The ability to self-express enables them to have healthy relationships where they can communicate well and attentively listen to others.

Praying with your children sets an example of spirituality and faith for them. By spiritually leading through example, you strengthen your children's trust in God and also your relationship with them. In the future, their memories of shared prayer time might bring them comfort and strength, and they may pray with your grandchildren. The strong familial relationships that form through shared prayer will be a rock to cling to when worldly temptations arise.

The Benefits of Starting Young

Establishing a Routine

Making prayer a daily activity helps it become an indispensable part of everyday life. Once prayer becomes part of a routine, we (including children) miss it when it is skipped. Children respond well to the structure and predictability that a routine brings, and they will quickly regard prayer time as a natural part of the day. How wonderful that connecting with our God can become such an integral part of our lives!

Having a routine, whether it is a fixed bedtime, making their beds before school, or praying before meals, helps children feel secure in a trusted structure and develop self-discipline. Appreciating the value of structure and planning, as well as having self-discipline, sets children on the road to success in many areas of their lives. They will faithfully spend time with God, study for tests and do all their homework, diligently attend sports practice, and later in life, be trusted employees or employers who can plan their tasks well and execute them to completion.

One of the ways you can help your children learn self-discipline and stick to routines is to have a set prayer schedule. The schedule should be fun and make prayer something to look forward to. If prayer is made a burden, it can turn a child away from God.

Prayer Routine After Something Bad Happened

Be kind and understanding if a child is angry at God and doesn't want to talk to Him after something bad happens. This response is natural, as children's faith can be so strong that they believe God will answer any prayer in the expected way. When something bad happens, such as the death of a pet, illness, or even losing a favorite toy, a child's heart can be too broken to want to praise God, and the child can't yet fully understand that God's plan includes hardship and heartbreak. In these cases, reassure your child by telling them that God has a plan for all things and that the pet is playing with God in Heaven now and will be returned when the child is in Heaven too, one day far in the future, or that God allowed the toy to get lost so that a sad child may find it, or that God allows illness as part of nature. Then, lead the child in a short prayer to say thank you for the time they had with the pet, and add something special about the pet, such as "Dear God, thank you for all the happiness and love Spot gave us. Please give Spot her favorite treats every day. We look forward to playing with Spot in Heaven one day. Amen."

Starting prayer young can be an enormous source of comfort for a child. Prayer gives them a place to turn to when the world feels confusing or painful.

Laying the Foundation

Childhood experiences shape the person we become. Children exposed to prayer from an early age have a foundation on which they can build their faith and foster a strong personal relationship with God. They are blessed to have God as their friend and protector while they grow and His guidance during their formative years.

Join me in the next chapter, where we'll discuss designated prayer spaces, incorporating prayer into daily routines, the use of visual aids, symbols, and interactive tools in an age-appropriate way to enhance prayer, and prayer as a family activity.

Chapter 2

CREATING A PRAYERFUL ENVIRONMENT

Now that we know why children should pray and how you can introduce prayer into their daily routine, let's explore some ways you can cultivate an atmosphere conducive to prayer, especially suited for children.

Designating a Prayer Space

We have special places in our homes for all sorts of things, depending on their function. For instance, we work with papers, books, and computers at a desk, not in the bath, and cook in the kitchen, not in the bedroom. Everything in its place and a place for everything! This also applies to prayer. Although we can pray anytime and anywhere to our God, who is everywhere all the time, children may need a special place away from distractions. Such a designated prayer place also helps children understand the concepts of holiness and sacredness as being set apart for God. In this section, we'll explore how to make and maintain a prayer space.

Location, Location, Location

Realtors know that differences in prices of identical houses come down to location. People want to live where they feel safe; are close to doctors, shops, and schools; and where the streets are clean and well-maintained. When making a prayer space, we can follow the realtor's rule that location makes all the difference.

What to look for in the ideal prayer space location:

- You don't need an entire room, but you do need enough space for your family to stand, kneel, or sit together. If you make a prayer space for individual private prayer, make sure there is enough room for one person to pray comfortably without feeling cramped. In other words, if you plan to convert a closet into a prayer space where you'll join the children for family prayer time, make sure it can fit everybody without having to contort yourself. Getting cramps or going numb will definitely distract from the prayer!

- The space should be well-lit. Many children are instinctively afraid of the dark. This was a survival mechanism in the days when our ancestors could be threatened by predators if they ventured outside at night. Although predators are no longer a threat, the fear remains, and it isn't anything to be ashamed of. God made children afraid of the dark to keep them safe! Keep this fear in mind and make sure your prayer area isn't dark and scary for a child. You can't expect a child to open up to God in a spirit of joyful worship when they are scared that a monster might jump out and snatch them.

- Choose a prayer space that is as quiet and far away from distractions as possible. If your prayer space is in the garden, make sure that it isn't on top of an ant nest or near a mosquito hotspot. Keep the climate in mind and have a backup prayer space for winter or bad weather. Preferably, the backup space should be comfortable, quiet, and warm enough to allow you to pray without clattering teeth, shivering, or hearing every raindrop loudly on the roof.

- If you are pressed for space, you can make a portable prayer space. Put your Bible, Bible story coloring books, prayer request journal, and devotional items such as crosses and crucifixes in a toolbox, basket, or wheeled cart. Then you can quickly convert your kitchen table or living room into a family prayer space and have a convenient place to put all your children's religious items.

- The goal of a prayer space is just to have a dedicated area for prayer, so it really doesn't need to take a lot of space or have fancy decorations. Even a special chair or a corner of the garage will do! If you don't have any space to spare, you can use a special prayer blanket or rug that you can lay on the floor to instantly transform it into a prayer space and easily roll it up and out of the way when not in use.

Decorating the Prayer Space

A prayer space should be inviting and fun. Here are some tipson how to make sure your prayer space isn't dreary, with the added bonus of combining education with decoration:

- Combine prayer with education by having a globe or a world map in the prayer space. When you include prayers for blessings, help, and protection for missionaries or people who suffered a disaster in another country, your children can learn the location of the country.

- Allow your children to help decorate the prayer space. They can draw pictures of biblical characters or scenes or write their favorite Bible verses. You can put them up on the wall with painter's tape, which won't damage the wall or the paintwork.

- Perhaps you can put up a cork board for prayer requests or an erasable whiteboard. This will also come in handy for teaching Bible stories or during Bible study with older children.

Maintaining the Sanctity

Even if the prayer space is only an old rug and a few Bible verses stuck to the wall, it is still a place dedicated to the worship of the Almighty God, and thus, it is the same as a temple. Just as we are reverent and respectful in church, we need to be the same in the prayer space. Help your children maintain the sanctity of the prayer space with these guidelines:

- Very young children may feel more comfortable if they have a special stuffed animal that they can imagine is praying with them. *This is fine!* Our heavenly Father understands that children sometimes need this kind of extra security. After all, as adults, we occasionally need extra comfort too. Stuffed animals will not make prayer or the prayer space any less sacred.

- King David praised God with song and dance, and it found favor in the eyes of God. Our Lord doesn't mind a joyful noise! Your children can sing off-key, keep an off-beat with a tambourine, or dance clumsily in praise. Your prayer space will remain dedicated to God even if your children have no musical talent.

- When it is time to pray, children should be focused only on prayer. Explain to them that prayer time isn't playtime. The prayer space and prayer time are set apart for God and godly things, meaning that they are sacred.

- Teach them that prayer is God's time and that it is disrespectful to make noise or otherwise distract people when they are praying.

- Explain to your children that some things are private. This doesn't mean they are secret, but it does mean that they aren't everybody's business. Sometimes, people request prayer but they don't want everyone to know what they are struggling with. What the family prays for in the prayer space and who they are praying for is private. Remind your children that part of keeping the sanctity of prayer is to respect other people's privacy. Don't be a blabbermouth about prayer.

Incorporating Prayer Into Daily Routines

In this section, we'll look at some ideas on how to make prayer part of a child's daily activities. Once prayer becomes routine, it will be consistent and a natural part of everyday life.

Morning Prayers

Many people like kicking off the day with something energizing, such as an early morning run, a refreshing shower, a solid breakfast, or a strong cup of coffee. Just as our bodies enjoy a morning jolt, our spirits also like starting the day on a positive note. What better way than to focus on our loving Father to set the tone for the day?

Here are some ideas for starting the day with spiritual nourishment:

- Children who are old enough for private prayer can do so right after waking up. The prayer doesn't have to be elaborate; it can be a simple "Bless this day dear Lord, and keep us safe and sound. Lead me to walk in your ways. Amen."

- After breakfast and before leaving for school is the perfect time for morning family prayer. Use your designated prayer area or sit together at the breakfast table. Lead the family prayer and have the children repeat after you, or simply say "amen" with you after the prayer. A prayer asking for God's blessings, protection, and guidance over the family, friends, and teachers will be suitable.

- If you have older children, pay attention to what they do at school. Take note of upcoming tests, sporting events, or things that cause them to worry, and incorporate these things into your prayers. This will personalize your prayers and reassure your children that both God and you are involved in their lives and actively listen to their concerns. For example, if your child is scared or worried after seeing images of war on the news, pray that God will protect His people and bring peace to troubled lands. For tests, you can ask God to help your children keep a clear, calm mind. For sporting events, dedicate the event to God and pray that the winners remain humble and thankful to God for their athletic talents, while the losers show grace and thankfulness for the opportunity to learn and improve. Personalized prayers will also help keep fidgety youngsters' attention on the prayers!

Saying Grace

Also known as mealtime blessings, saying grace is an opportunity to express gratitude for the food on the table. Don't forget to also ask for God's blessings on the farmer who cultivated the food, the parent or caregiver who worked hard to buy it, and the person who prepared the meal.

Asking God's blessing over a meal teaches children to appreciate the work and investment that go into growing, earning, providing, and preparing food. It makes children aware that having enough to eat is a blessing and a privilege. This awareness leads to a sense of gratitude and dependency upon God as the provider of blessings.

Saying grace before and after meals soon becomes routine. While it is wonderful to make God part of a daily routine, be mindful that saying grace over a meal doesn't turn into a quick rumble that is thoughtlessly said with the focus merely on starting the meal instead of honoring God.

Bedtime Prayer

A few private minutes before bedtime prayer is an ideal opportunity to evaluate the day and seek God's guidance on where we may have strayed from His will and how we can do better tomorrow. This reflection should not aim to make children neurotic perfectionists who fear making mistakes but instead inspire them to do their best and to forgive themselves and others when mistakes are made.

Right before going to bed, children can pray for God's protection during sleep. Having bedtime prayer as a nightly ritual can help children settle down and fall asleep more easily.

Visual Aids

Children generally love color and pictures. They prefer illustrated Bible stories to the text-only Bibles of their parents. Images and symbols grab their attention and stimulate their imaginations. Their ability to grasp abstract concepts isn't fully developed yet, but visual aids can help them comprehend aspects of faith such as forgiveness, prayer, and salvation.

Most toy stores have small plastic animals that are perfect visual aids for the story of Noah and the Ark. You can even stretch the story over a couple of days and add a pair of animals every day. As an added bonus, the animals can also double as barn animals and wild, adoring animals for a Christmas nativity scene.

Colorful, child-oriented videos that depict Bible stories are entertaining and teach children religious principles in age-appropriate ways.

Symbolic Objects

Symbols tell stories that can be understood without the ability to read, making them ideal teaching tools for very young children.

Children don't fully understand the agony that Jesus endured on the cross (which is good; children would be traumatized if they fully realized the extent of His suffering), but they can and do recognize the cross as a symbol of Jesus dying for our sins. Older children may want to wear a cross around their necks as a tangible reminder of their faith.

The Holy Spirit may be too abstract for children to grasp. However, they have all seen doves and can relate to this symbol as representing something coming down from Heaven.

Candles are symbolic of God lighting our way. If your children are old enough to handle matches responsibly, you can have them light a candle to shine during prayer time to symbolize God's guidance.

Interactive Tools

Here are some ways in which interactive tools can help your children in their spiritual development:

- Flashcards can help them memorize prayers and Bible verses.

- Puzzles and riddles are fun ways to stimulate the memory.

- Children love stories! Interactive story time, where you show them the illustrations as you go along and ask questions related to the story, will be sure to keep their attention.

- Biblical-themed activities are a practical way to make the past come alive. Children can make baskets (paint some old buckets) in remembrance of Moses, gather long grass (which become sheaves of wheat with a bit of imagination) to imitate Ruth, and make paper crowns for King David.

- Children are natural actors who love putting on a show. Let them drape themselves in old sheets or blankets, use your garden rake as a staff, and draw beards with child-friendly face paint (it washes off easily) to get into character. Acting out a Bible story will not only help them remember the story but also understand the lesson behind it.

- Older children might prefer to use their own prayer journals instead of a prayer request taped against a wall. The journal should be for their own eyes only, since it contains their private conversations with the Lord.

Making Prayer a Family Activity

Getting together to share prayer bonds a family in a close, spiritual way. Shared faith, values, and goals make every family member feel part of a team that has each other's backs. Let's explore some ideas on how to establish prayer time to make it a special family tradition.

The Value of Family Prayer

When a family gets together for prayer, Bible study, or praise and worship, they act as a support system for each other. Family members who share the same faith are there to encourage each other and help each other find their way back when they stray from God's Word. The family prayer circle provides a safe, spiritually nurturing space to talk about concerns, reflect upon events, and share insights and wisdom.

Listening to other family members talk about their daily struggles and joys develops children's sense of compassion. They come to realize that other people also have burdens and worries, and they learn to share joy without jealousy. The children become more sensitive to the needs of others and learn how to be supportive.

Establishing a Prayer Tradition

When something becomes a family tradition, children and grandchildren will look forward to participating, and many warm memories will be shared about it. A prayer tradition can bond a family even more strongly than the family tradition of Grandma's Thanksgiving pudding, which she learned from her grandmother. Just like the pudding, family prayer tradition is something special to be shared only with the family and, perhaps on special occasions, with a guest or two.

To establish your family's own prayer tradition, you have to set realistic goals. With children in the house, it is unrealistic to expect an hour of silent contemplation before prayer or for the children to memorize complicated Bible verses or long prayers. Let's face it, prayer time will probably be 10 minutes of singing a devotional song and a short prayer. That's fine! With repetition, the song and prayer will become a spiritual hug of comfort and encouragement.

What makes something a tradition is consistent repetition. Of course, there may be circumstances that cause family prayer time to be skipped, such as illness or disaster, but as long as the prayer time is done as consistently as possible, it will become a tradition.

Before deciding on when, where, and what to pray for your family tradition, experiment first. Try your family prayer space, the breakfast table, the front door before everyone leaves for the morning, or other places where everyone will be together at the same time. Experiment with various times for prayer, as young children are sometimes simply too full of energy or too tired to focus on prayer. Older children might be too distracted in the evenings when they are tired from sports and still have to study or do homework. Morning prayer could also be too stressful and cause the children to be late for school. Keep experimenting until your family finds the right fit.

Now that you know how to make a dedicated prayer space, what to put in it, and how to make family prayer a tradition that will last for generations to come, we move on to the next chapter for ideas on how to teach children to pray.

Chapter 3

TEACHING CHILDREN HOW TO PRAY

In this chapter, we'll focus on practical steps to help children incorporate meaningful, effective prayer into their spiritual development.

Leading by Example

The key to teaching children how to pray is to lead by example. For the same reason it isn't a good idea to use a swear word near children, it is important for them to see and hear you pray. Children imitate adults; it is how they learn.

If you have a prayer routine, your children will have the example of dedicated prayer, and they'll understand that prayer is a daily discipline, not merely a few words whenever they need a miracle. Children who are familiar with prayer can more easily make it part of their way of life.

Not only the timing but also the content of your prayers is important. Your children need to observe you praying for others in order to learn how to be considerate of other people's struggles. Only praying for your own needs sends the message that prayer is little more than personal wish-fulfillment.

Also, when children hear you pray for them, they are reassured of your love and know that you care about their physical and spiritual well-being. This can be an immense source of comfort and can encourage your children to share their problems with you because they know you will help and lead them in prayers for guidance.

It isn't enough to set a spiritual example only through prayer. Your life has to be in line with God's will as set out in His Word; otherwise, your child might later view prayer as a hypocritical action. Make sure your life follows these rules as closely as possible, while recognizing that everyone falls short and that God forgives our trespasses if we repent:

- Be kind, generous, patient, and honest.

- Have self-control over your actions and words.

- Be ethical and compassionate in all aspects of your life. Yes, that includes being compassionate to people who are rude to you!

- Base your values on the fruits of the spirit rather than on money and possessions.

- Help others with a spirit of joy and community. When children see you joyfully helping your spouse, assisting a neighbor, or volunteering at a shelter, they are more likely to follow your example, perform their chores, and do kind deeds to please God and not for material rewards.

- Stand up for your beliefs. Children who have the example of a parent who isn't afraid to do or say what is right instead of what is popular are more likely to resist peer pressure.

- Admit when you've made a mistake, ask forgiveness, and make amends.

Always remember that your children will imitate you. Set them a worthy example in every part of your life.

Letting Children Participate

It lays a strong spiritual foundation for your children if you let them observe you pray, praise, and worship. After observation comes the practice. Advance your children to practical prayer by letting them take part in family prayer time or allowing them to say grace before or after a meal.

Participating in prayer lets your children feel included in something important and can contribute to an even stronger bond with your children. Sharing the deep spiritual connection that only sincere prayer can bring lets your children feel safe, loved, and valued.

Allow your children to ask questions when you read them Bible stories. Ask them questions in return to gauge their understanding.

Reflecting on Benefits

We've already discussed the benefits of starting young with prayer, so let's have a quick look at how teaching children to pray can benefit your adult spiritual journey.

Teaching a child the principles of prayer reminds you of how important it is to stick to the basics. Prayer only requires a sincere heart, not the latest fad book or an obscure prayer from the Old Testament against the Philistines. Your child looks at faith through fresh, innocent eyes, and this can inspire you to simplify your own spiritual practices. Do you really need to pray for all the material things on your list? Are you truly approaching God in a sincere, humble manner? Is your relationship with the Heavenly Father a model for your relationship with your children?

Taking time to compare the prayer life of an innocent child with your own prayers may lead to introspection that can strengthen the bond with your family, community, and God.

Child-Appropriate Teaching

A young child will have difficulty understanding abstract concepts such as spiritual salvation, original sin, and selflessness. Explain spiritual concepts in ways appropriate to their age, using language they are familiar with.

Before you teach your child how to connect with God, you first need to discuss who God is and why we pray to Him.

Children aged 2–4 have very short attention spans and very little experience of the world, so keep your teaching simple and short. Let them look at the pictures in an illustrated Bible, and if you can, read the stories using different voices for the characters. You can also act out some Bible stories with dolls and stuffed animals. At this age, prayer should mostly be about God's love. Thanking God for their blessings, such as family, a warm bed, pets, and food, lays a strong foundation for deeper prayer as they get older.

Between the ages of 5–8, children can understand concepts such as forgiveness and promises. They are also capable of memorizing short Bible verses. Appropriate prayer would focus on God's protection, forgiveness, and unconditional love.

Children between the ages of 9 and 12 begin to understand more complex concepts such as temptation, courage, and context. They become aware that the culture and practices of the Bible, especially the Old Testament, are not always appropriate in modern times. For example, the Bible didn't address slavery, but today we know that it is wrong. During this age group, children may also start questioning the basic Biblical concepts that they've been told so far. Expect questions such as "Who created God?" and "Why do God let bad things happen?" We'll discuss some potential answers to the tough questions later in this chapter.

Talent Shows and Art

When something is fun, it is easier to learn. Have a Sunday night talent show at home where your children (and perhaps their friends and cousins too) can perform scenes from the Bible and recite Bible verses. At the end of the show, when the children are relaxed and comfortable in front of their appreciative audience, each child can say a prayer. This helps children develop the confidence to pray out loud in front of others, which is useful in prayer circles, family prayer time, and perhaps one day standing in the ministry.

To help children articulate exactly what they are praying for, let them draw pictures. If they are going to pray for peace, their drawings will let you see if they truly understand what peace means. Their drawings will also show you things that are important in their lives that they can't yet verbalize.

Relatable Scenarios

Use real-life examples to explain to children when and what to pray. Discussing current events is an excellent opportunity to talk to your children about praying for peace and guidance. Even small local events can be suitable for teaching. Imagine sitting on the bleachers at a school baseball game when one of the children gets hurt. You can discreetly say a quick prayer asking for God's healing hand over the injured child. Your children will then see prayer in action and realize that prayer isn't only for the home and church.

Life happens, and frustrating events can be turned into prayer. If your car won't start, call your children and tell them that you are frustrated and worried that you'll be late for work. Let them know that annoying things happen to everyone, but God expects us to behave in a way pleasing to Him, even when we want to scream and shout and be rude. Then, lead your family in a prayer asking God to give you calm, patience, and peace of mind. (Consider reading the story of Job to your children before bed.) Teaching your children that God is in control and only a prayer away will lead them to trust Him for all their needs.

The Tough Questions About God

One question that bothers both children and many adults is *why bad things can happen to people who trust God to bless and protect them*. Being bullied at school, seeing disasters or wars on TV, or having something tragic or traumatic happen to them can make children lose faith in God as a loving, omnipotent, and caring Father. Explain to your children that the world is in a fallen condition due to the decisions of people. God allows people to have free will, and that is the ability to make both good and evil choices. Sometimes God intervenes with a miracle, and other times He allows things to happen for reasons we can't understand. Our minds are tiny compared to God's, who can see all things across time and space. Reassure your child that there are many occasions where God intervenes, but we don't know about them. For example, God can make parents or the bus driver get stuck in traffic so that they don't get in an accident that is about to happen a block away. So, even though God knows the children may get in trouble for being late to school, He allows it for a greater purpose. When bad things happen, children can and should turn to God for comfort because He understands what happened and why it had to happen, and being a loving God, His heart breaks when His earthly children suffer.

Children don't have a sophisticated understanding of time and, as a result, may not grasp the concept of eternity in the same way adults do. Children might struggle to comprehend the eternal nature of God. Don't be surprised if they ask you when God was born, or if God made us, who made God? You might attempt to explain God's timelessness by telling your children that forever goes on and on without end, not only in the direction of the future but also in the past. At prayer time, your children can ask God to help them understand that He has no beginning or end.

It is natural to wonder if God really exists. After all, we can't see Him and have to put our faith in a 2,000-year-old book. As children age, they might become skeptical about God's existence and give up on prayer. The easiest way to prove the existence of our Creator is to look at His creation. Talk to your children about the complexity and beauty of the earth and all things on it. Should your children counteract with claims about evolution, you can search online for the various rebuttals and explain to them that evolution is merely a theory and thus unproven. If your children are more comfortable with the idea of evolution, ask them to consider whether it is possible that God used evolution to create the world—after all, if they can believe in an unproven theory, they can also believe in the "theory" that God created everything in the manner of His choosing. In prayer, your children can ask God to guide them toward proof of His existence.

Traditional Prayers

The old favorite prayers of our ancestors link us and our children to our family and community and provide a sense of cultural connection. We become part of a tradition of believers that can stretch hundreds, if not thousands, of years into the past. Traditional prayers help us realize that we are part of a continuous faith community. In this section, we'll look at some traditional prayers that are suitable for children or family prayer time.

If you are Catholic, you can teach your very young children the *sign of the cross*. The children get used to thinking of God as a Trinity, and when they cross themselves, it reinforces the concept of their bodies as holy temples.

The next prayer that Catholic children learn is the *Hail Mary*. This prayer is easy to learn with repetition.

Christian children of all denominations and churches learn the *Lord's Prayer (Our Father)*. Children from about age 10 and upwards can learn this prayer through regular repetition.

A traditional prayer suitable for everyone aged 10 and above focuses on giving *God the glory* for all our deeds. Here is the traditional prayer (Birch, n.d.):

> When we walk with you in the light of your love, it is your glory seen, not ours. When we minister to people in need, it is your hands that heal, not ours. When we talk of you to those whom we meet, it is your words that speak, not ours. When we worship you and offer our lives, your name is glorified, always.

Teenage children going through a hard time may find solace in *Reinhold Niebuhr's Serenity Prayer*. The first four lines of this prayer are well-known, but few people have heard the prayer in its entirety (Editor in Chief, 2019).

Psalm 23 (The Lord is my shepherd) is a wonderful prayer for all occasions and is easy to learn with regular repetition for elementary school children and older.

Exploring Different Prayer Formats

Some children love reciting old favorite prayers, while others prefer spur-of-the-moment prayers or call-and-response formats. To help your children find the prayer format that resonates best with their individual communication styles, let's look at some prayer formats.

Having *fixed times for prayer* disciplines you to organize your day around God and your spiritual development, rather than squeezing a little prayer time into your busy schedule. This prayer format isn't practical for everyone, but if you can do it, it places God at the top of your daily priorities.

Fasting isn't prayer per se, but it can form part of a special prayer where you give up something, such as food, for a short while. Children can fast too, but the fasting period should never be more than an hour or two, and they should always have access to as much water as they want. For small children, delaying dinner by an hour as part of fasting is fine.

Music has the power to move us in ways that dry text can't. Music that expresses a connection to God is prayer! Sing along (silently is fine if you are self-conscious or have vocal problems) and dedicate the lyrics to God. The music can be hymns, gospel music, or your own composition. If you are like me and lack any musical talent but still want to compose something as a personal prayer, pick a song you know and make up your own words of prayer. For a very young child, even the nursery song *The Wheels on the Bus Go Round and Round*" (*The Wheels on the Bus*, n.d.) can be a musical prayer if they sing *The love of God goes round and round.*

If you are praying over a certain area, a *prayer walk* can enhance the experience. For example, hold your child's hand as you walk through your house and ask for God's blessing in every room. You can consider praying something like "Dear

God, please protect us while we sleep in the bedrooms, and "Dear God, thank you for the blessing of food" in the kitchen. Older children might want to do a prayer walk around their school or church to ask God's protection, guidance, and blessing.

Silent prayer is more than merely praying in your head. You need to silence your racing thoughts and mentally block distractions so that you can listen for God's answer in your heart.

Contemplative prayer involves stilling the mind and simply being with God. We often focus so much on being busy in the material world that we seldom take time to listen to what God is saying to us. During contemplative prayer, God speaks to us through the Holy Spirit, which usually isn't in the form of words but rather through inspiration, a sense of holiness, or an awareness of God's will.

Circle or conversational prayer involves a group of people taking turns to pray short prayers about a specific need. For example, if the prayer topic is seeking guidance, one person might pray a sentence or two asking God to guide them in a new career, while the next person might pray for guidance in making the right decision regarding a personal matter. This type of prayer brings a closer sense of community and shared burdens.

People who might be uncomfortable praying in a group but still want the support of a fellow believer can pray with a *prayer buddy*. The buddy can be anyone willing to take a minute to share a prayer, but having a permanent prayer buddy offers an opportunity to build a special friendship with spiritual foundations. A prayer buddy doesn't have to be physically present; a shared prayer over the phone or via text will do.

If you are at a loss for words, you can turn to the *psalms* and pray the words of King David. All you have to do is find a psalm that expresses what you have difficulty saying and read it to God. God knows your heart and intentions, and He inspired David to write the psalms, knowing they would be a comfort and help for many people to come.

Spontaneous Prayer

We don't have to wait for a specific prayer time to talk to God. Things happen around and to us all the time that we want to tell God. There is an ample opportunity for spontaneous prayer in everyone's life, especially for children, who are by nature more impulsive and present in the moment.

Teach your children by example to pray for God's healing and comfort for people in an ambulance when you hear sirens pass by. When you see something particularly beautiful, such as a butterfly or the first buds of spring, call your children to have a look and praise God together.

Tell your children that God is always listening and wants us to make Him part of our everyday life. God loves us and is always interested in His children's experiences, thoughts, and emotions.

In the next chapter, we'll discuss prayer on special occasions, such as birthdays and holidays.

Chapter 4

PRAYING AT SPECIAL OCCASIONS

Let's take a look at the importance of prayer during various special occasions and provide examples you can teach your children.

Why Pray on Special Occasions?

We love to celebrate the milestones of our lives with parties, photos, and phone calls to loved ones. God is a major part of our lives, and it is His blessings that make these milestones possible, so He should be part of our special occasions. Acknowledging God during special times encourages children to realize the important role our Heavenly Father has in our lives and fosters a sense of humility and gratitude.

Prayer connects the spiritual with our worldly achievements, bringing a deeper meaning to our lives.

The Special Occasions

The following examples of special occasion prayers are arranged from simple to advanced, so you can choose prayers that are age-appropriate for your children. These prayers are merely ideas or templates that you can add to or change as you like.

Birthday Prayers

A birthday is an occasion where we can express gratitude for God's gift of life for another year. Birthday prayers help your children make God part of their joy and celebration.

If it is the child's birthday:

"Dear God, thank You for another year. I love You. Amen."

"Dear God, thank You for keeping and blessing me, and please be with me in the next year of my life and all my days. Amen."

"Dear God, may the joyful birthday candles reflect the light of Your presence in my life. Thank You for all Your blessings in every day of my life. I pray in Jesus' name. Amen."

If it is someone else's birthday:

"Dear God, please make (name's) birthday happy. I love You. Amen."

"Dear God, please bless (name) with love and happiness on their birthday and every day after. Amen."

"Dear God, thank You for keeping and blessing (name), and please spare (name) for many years to come. Please let Your light of love and joy shine over (him/her) today and every day. I pray in Jesus' name. Amen."

Prayer at the Start of a School Year

A new school year can be equally scary and exciting. A prayer lets your children turn to God to steady their nerves and start the year with the intention of always trying their best.

"Dear God, please bless my school, teachers, and schoolmates and help us do our best. Amen."

"Dear God, please bless everyone in my school and let all my work be to Your glory. Amen."

"Dear God, please bless our school so that everyone in it may come to believe and trust in You. Please guide me to be an example to others of what a believer should be. Remind me that all my efforts are for Your glory. I pray in Jesus' name. Amen."

Prayer at the End of a School Year

When the last school bell rings for the year, children usually think only of the freedom that a holiday brings. A short prayer of thanks for the past year and blessings for the holiday reminds your children that God never leaves their side.

"Dear God, thank You for being with us through the year. Please bless us during the holiday. Amen."

"Dear God, thank You for Your blessings throughout the year. Please keep Your hand over all students, staff, and their families during the holiday. Amen."

"Dear God, thank You for Your presence in my life and for inspiring me to do my best and may all students and staff return to school refreshed and rested. I pray in Jesus' name. Amen."

Prayer Before Tests or Exams

Children want to do well at school, but sometimes their nerves cause their minds to go blank. A prayer will help settle them down with the knowledge that God is with them.

"Dear God, please help me do my best today. Amen."

"Dear God, please focus my mind on doing my best so that I may honor Your Name. "Amen.

"Dear God, please bless my mindset and memory so that I may honor Your Name with my best effort. I pray in Jesus' name. Amen."

Prayer After Tests or Exams

Many children and college students pray for God's help before a test but forget to thank Him for His help afterward. These prayers of thanks remind your children that good manners also include thanking God.

"Dear God, thank You for being with me. Amen."

"Dear God, thank You for helping me do my best. May my efforts be for Your glory. Amen."

"Dear God, thank You for blessing me with a good education. May my efforts always honor Your Holy Name. I pray in Jesus' name. Amen."

Prayers for Soldiers

These prayers can be a great comfort for children who have a family member serving the country or who feel afraid after seeing war on TV.

"Dear God, please bless our soldiers and keep them safe. Amen."

"Dear God, please hold Your hand over our soldiers and grant us peace soon. Amen."

"Dear God, please keep Your hand over our armed forces and everyone who works to keep us safe. Please comfort the families of fallen warriors. May Your peace be with us. I pray in Jesus' name. Amen."

Prayer for the President

Even if the president isn't who you voted for or makes decisions that you disagree with, we still have to "give to Caesar what is Caesar's" and acknowledge that leading a country is not an easy job. The best way to make the country turn to God is to pray for leaders who follow His will.

"Dear God, please bless the president with wisdom. Amen."

"Dear God, please guide our president in wisdom and strength to do Your will. Amen."

"Dear God, please guide the president to walk in Your righteousness and to be always mindful that he is a servant of God and of everyone in this country. I pray in Jesus' name. Amen."

Prayers for Easter

Small children may not fully understand the significance of the crucifixion and resurrection. Their minds aren't developed enough to understand death. For this reason, it is better to focus on Jesus cleansing our sins instead of the crucifixion. Besides, graphic descriptions of His suffering can upset little ones, and such details can wait until they are older.

"Dear God, thank You that Jesus made my heart pure. Amen."

"Dear God, thank You that Jesus carried our sins. Please help me live in such a way that Jesus will one day welcome me in Heaven. Amen."

"Dear God, I am humbled and grateful for the sacrifice of Jesus. Please remind me every day that Jesus lives in my heart and His blood saved me. In Jesus' name, I pray. Amen."

Prayers for Christmas

Christmas has been so commercialized that children might think Christmas is about Santa Claus and presents. Christmas prayers remind them of the reason for festivity.

"Happy birthday, Jesus! I love You. Amen."

"Dear God, thank You for Your love and that You sent Jesus to save us. Please bless our Christmas with joy. Amen."

"Dear God, thank You for loving us so much that You sent Jesus. Please guide us to make Jesus the true reason for our Christmas celebration. I pray in Jesus' name. Amen."

Prayers for Baptism

Children whose siblings or cousins are getting baptized, or who are themselves getting baptized, can mark this very special event with prayer. These prayers are suitable for the baptism of infants or older children.

"Dear God, please bless (name's) baptism. Amen."

"Dear God, thank You for the baptism that cleanses (name) of sin. Amen."

"Dear God, please bless (name) and thank You for letting us be Your children who are cleansed of sin. I pray in Jesus' name. Amen."

Prayers for the Sick

God has the power to heal sickness, and children understand that. It is a beautiful act of faith when a child prays for healing. Sometimes, however, God chooses not to heal someone and let them remain sick, allow the illness to get worse, or take them to Heaven. If the sick person or animal doesn't get better after prayer, children may feel guilty and think they didn't pray hard enough or that they did something wrong. In such cases, please explain to your children that God did hear their prayers, but He has a greater plan that we may not fully understand.

"Dear God, please help (name) get healthy. Amen."

"Dear God, as part of Your greater plan, please let (name) get well. Amen."

"Dear God, I pray that You will be with (name) and ease their pain. If it is Your will, please heal (him/her) and restore (him/her) to full health. I pray in Jesus' name. Amen."

Prayers When Someone Has Died

Children may not always understand the finality of death, but they do suffer heartbreak when someone they love (whether human or animal) suddenly isn't there anymore. These prayers may be a source of comfort for them.

"Dear God, I love and miss (name). Please keep (him/her) safe until we meet again in Heaven. Amen."

"Dear God, my heart is so sore. I miss (name) very much. I know we'll be together again in Heaven, but until then, I need your comfort. Amen."

"Dear God, thank You for the privilege of knowing (name). May the memories of (him/her) always bring joy until we are reunited in Heaven. Please send Your love and comfort to me and everyone who is mourning this loss. I pray in Jesus' name. Amen."

Prayers When Someone Is Divorced

It is a sad reality of life that relationships don't always work out. Children are prone to blame themselves in these circumstances, and they are uncertain and fearful of what happens next. Helping them pray when divorce is on the horizon allows them to understand that God will be with them no matter what.

"Dear God, thank You that my mommy will always be my mommy and my daddy will always be my daddy, even if we live in different houses. Amen."

"Dear God, I am worried and scared for the future. Please help my heart realize that divorce isn't my fault and that I am still loved. Amen."

"Dear God, please help me deal with the big changes in our family in a loving, understanding, and respectful way, and let Your love for all of us be a source of strength and comfort. I pray in Jesus' name. Amen."

Prayers for When the Family Is Struggling Financially

Your finances are private, and children don't have to know the details, but young ones can tell something is amiss when they suddenly have to give up extracurricular activities and have to scale down on other things. A kind explanation that money isn't as plentiful as before and that everyone in the family has to do with a little less for the time being is sufficient. God understands all our struggles, including financial ones, and we can turn to Him in prayer.

"Dear God, I am grateful for everything we have. Amen."

"Dear God, I am thankful for all Your blessings, but we can do with extra help. Please bless my family with opportunities. Amen."

"Dear God, I am troubled. My family is struggling, and I don't know how to help. Please guide us toward opportunities and bless us financially as You bless us with Your love. I pray in Jesus' name. Amen."

Prayers for Father's and Mother's Day

The role of a parent in a child's life can't be understated. As a parent, your nurturing, providing, teaching, and guidance make you an earthly reflection of our Heavenly Father. Live up to that responsibility with love, patience, kindness, and faith, and you'll be blessed with children who are happy that you're their Mom or Dad.

"Dear God, thank You for my (Mommy/Daddy). Amen."

"Dear God, thank You for my (Mom/ Dad). Please bless (her/ him) and keep (her/ him) safe. Amen."

"Dear God, thank You for the gift that is my (Mom/Dad). Please bless (her/him) with your love and guidance, and may we have (her/him) with us for many more happy years to come. I pray in Jesus' name. Amen."

Prayers for Forgiveness

We all make mistakes, and for the little ones, their guilt can be as innocent and big as their love and good intentions. These prayers will help them repent, learn from their mistakes, take responsibility, and dry their tears.

"Dear God, I am very sorry for (transgression). Amen."

"Dear God, I am sorry for (transgression) and ask for forgiveness. Help me to make things right. Amen."

"Dear God, I repent and need forgiveness from You and anyone I've hurt. I chose to (transgression). Please lead me back to follow Your will. I pray in Jesus' name. Amen."

Prayers for Monsters Under the Bed

Most small children go through a stage where they are convinced that there are monsters or ghosts in their closets or under their beds. They become scared at bedtime, and getting them to settle down and go to sleep involves checking with flashlights. By incorporating prayer, you help children control their fears and teach them that God is all-powerful.

"Dear God, please keep me safe from the monsters and make them go away. Amen."

Let's move on to explore how prayer affects children's emotional well-being.

Chapter 5

PRAYER AND EMOTIONAL WELL-BEING

The spiritual growth that follows from prayer and a personal relationship with God spills over into our emotional state. In this chapter, we'll delve into the effects of prayer on children's emotional well-being. Let's start with the effects of stress on children's emotional well-being and how it can be managed.

The Effects of Stress on Children

Children experience stress too! Just because they don't have to worry about paying the bills, working for a cranky boss, cooking healthy meals for the whole family on a shoestring budget, or navigating traffic in rush hour doesn't mean they don't experience worry and frustration.

Long-term and intense stress can transform from ordinary stress, which our minds and bodies can handle, into toxic stress. Toxic stress causes our bodies to be flooded with adrenaline and cortisol, and these hormones can, just as in adults, cause emotional problems such as behavioral issues, anxiety, difficulty sleeping or sleeping too much, unexplained sadness, difficulty concentrating, and getting sick more easily.

Prayer to Cope With Stress

When adults experience stress, they can go for a drive, watch a favorite movie, or call a best friend for a laughter-filled conversation. Children don't have these outlets and have to deal with their daily stress in different ways. One outlet that works for adults and children alike is prayer.

Children who pray in private are likely to tell God things they might not tell you. For example, children might tell God that someone stole their lunch money but delay telling a parent because the bully threatened them with violence if they told anyone. Prayer can relieve the stress of being bullied and help children cope better emotionally, but sooner or later, they will need adult intervention.

Praying before a stressful event, such as a test or sports tryout, helps focus children's attention on God, and this distraction can serve to calm them down. For older children, prayer before and after stressful events helps put things in perspective. They come to realize that what seems like a big deal at the moment is a small thing in the eyes of our all-powerful God, and what seems like the end of the world is just a speck in the dust of time for our eternal God.

Supplementary Tools for Managing Stress

To manage childhood stress, you can use several methods in addition to prayer. A little distraction and activity go a long way in helping children calm down and refocus.

Exercise

When people feel frustrated, they might stomp their feet, pull their hair, face-palm, wave their fists in the air, slam doors, or storm off. The stressful emotion often manifests physically with an urge to move. You don't want your child to go on a destructive rampage to relieve their frustration, but you can find ways to use movement constructively to soothe their inner Godzilla. Exercise allows a child to release steam while being healthy for their growing body.

Here are some examples of physical exercises that can help release your child's frustrations:

- A park or backyard gives your child the opportunity to run and jump to their heart's content. A basketball hoop or a soccer ball can keep them busy for hours. A soft ball and a light plastic tennis racket, along with a wall to hit the ball against, will relieve frustration while improving their hand-eye coordination.

- If you don't have access to a playing area where your child can run around, you can let them jump rope in the bathroom or some other place where it is unlikely they'll knock anything over with the rope.

- Limited space doesn't mean no exercise. Jumping jacks, running in place, or dancing on the spot can help drain frustration from your child's muscles and distract them from the cause of their stress.

Breathing Techniques

Due to the effects of hormones, children under stress (including those throwing a temper tantrum!) experience automatic changes in breathing and heart rate. Their hearts race and they breathe shorter and shallower. This breathing pattern can lead to children feeling even more stressed and anxious. Deep breathing breaks this stress cycle by sending more oxygen to the brain, which helps bring back feelings of calm and slows the heart rate. Here are some breathing techniques your children can try when they feel stressed out:

- Help your children pick up feathers from a park or buy a few colored feathers from a craft shop (they are very inexpensive). Show them how to breathe deeply and slowly, as if they are smelling a flower or savoring the scent of a delicious meal. Then, instead of a regular exhale, have them blow slowly on the sides of the feather until their lungs are empty. Two of these breaths are enough for starters since it can cause dizziness for people not used to such deep and slow breathing. Your children can gradually increase the number of feather deep breaths as their lungs get used to it.

- Moving the arms up and down with breaths adds a little kinetic distraction for the stressed child, which, together with the deep breaths, can help calm them down quickly. You might feel silly when demonstrating this method to your children, but the fun and relaxation will make up for it. As you take a deep, slow breath, lift your arms until your lungs are full with your arms above your head. Then, lower your arms as you slowly exhale until your arms are at your sides and your lungs are empty. Repeat two or three times.

- Very young children will have lots of fun with raspberry breaths (and so will you when you show them how). Breathe in slowly, and as you exhale, blow a raspberry (put your tongue between your lips and let it vibrate as you exhale). Chances are, your children will soon be laughing their stress and tension away.

Arts and Crafts

Being creative is a gentle outlet and distraction that can keep children busy for hours. Paying attention to what your children make may help you find out the sources of their stress.

- Something as basic as a coloring book and crayons can help them forget what irritated them and restore their peace of mind.

- A little playdough can help children calm down in the same way that a stress ball helps adults. The physical act of fiddling with the squishy texture distracts from problems and worries. Also, some children are kinetic learners, which means that they concentrate better when they are allowed to fidget while listening to lessons.

- Children don't always have the vocabulary to express themselves, so making objects to represent the things that cause them stress can help them explain what bothers them. For example, a young child may draw or make a clay blob, and if you make up a story about the blob or drawing, it might reveal that the child made something to represent a "bad kid who calls me names" or "I'm sad because I don't like the school bus." Arts and crafts can give you the opportunity to dig for the root of your child's stress.

Building Resilience Through Prayer

Prayer enables us to face life's challenges with the courage and strength needed to get back after setbacks. This is what resilience is all about: the ability to bounce back.

In a spiritual sense, prayer plugs us into God's power so that we can draw strength and endurance directly from the Source. When we pray with the faith that God will heal, provide, or give a way out of difficult situations, we gain the courage to face another day. God will answer our prayers for help in His way, at His time, and according to His plan. When we don't see immediate answers to our prayers, God wants us to keep trusting and having faith in Him. This unshakable resilience in the face of adversity develops spiritual grit and tenacity.

Here are some ways that you can use prayer to build and maintain both your and your children's resilience:

- Make prayer such an integral part of your children's lives that they will automatically turn to God in times of trouble.

- Prayer in a group of believers, such as a family or prayer group, provides your children with a community that will encourage and support them when life gets hard.

- Regularly praying in a spirit of gratitude conditions the spirit and mind to find joy in what they already have, not in what they want to have. Focused attention on the present is called mindfulness, and when it is combined with sincere gratitude, every day becomes worthwhile.

- When our children pray for God to bless them with resilience, they need to realize that God may send tests and troubles on their paths. This is in answer to their prayers because the more we face and overcome trying times through our faith, the stronger we become. We don't grow stronger and more resilient by dealing only with small obstacles.

Emotional Regulation

We are born with basic emotional expressions such as crying and laughter, and as we grow, our emotions become more complex, and we have to adapt our emotional expressions. Although, as very young children, we cry or scream when we are unhappy, we have to learn how to regulate our emotions as part of the growing-up process. Emotional regulation is important to get along with others and to develop the self-control needed for personal growth.

Children have eight primary emotions, namely shame, fear, sadness, disgust, interest, surprise, joy, and anger. Other emotions and behaviors stem from these primary emotions. For example, anxiety may be rooted in fear, depression may stem from sadness, and violent behavior may arise from anger.

Secondary emotions are additional responses that build upon primary emotions, which are influenced by our experiences. For example, children who are punished when they express anger might develop anxiety on top of anger. Making fun of a child who is afraid can cause them to be ashamed the next time they feel fear. Because secondary emotions can arise from our reactions to our children's natural emotions, we should be careful to help them develop emotional regulation without invalidating their emotions, shaming them, or punishing them for their feelings.

Age-Appropriate Emotional Regulation

Infants have very basic needs, and therefore their emotions are instinctual attempts to get something they want, such as milk, a dry diaper, or being held, or to avoid something unpleasant, such as being hungry, uncomfortable, or alone. The best a baby can do to regulate their emotions is to indulge in self-soothing behaviors such as sucking their thumbs. If you have a fussy infant between six and nine months old, you might find that play songs such as *Itsy Bitsy Spider* and *Wheels on the Bus* calms their emotions more effectively and for a longer duration than talking to them or singing a lullaby. The effectiveness of using play songs to regulate infant emotions has been confirmed by a scientific study (Trehub et al., 2015)

Toddlers aren't soothed by playing songs anymore. They start to experience a wider range of emotions, which can be overwhelming for them, leading to tantrums, screaming fits, biting, and hitting. It is difficult to regulate emotions without knowing what they are, and parents should teach toddlers, starting from age three and upward, what emotions are called and why they feel them. This way, they learn that emotions are normal and that they have some measure of control over them. For example, when your toddler is angry because it is bedtime and they don't want to go to bed, you can help them understand their emotions by saying, "I know you are angry because you want to keep playing, but you can play again tomorrow when you are rested."

But be aware that children won't be able to fully understand all their emotions until about age 10, so be patient and have realistic expectations. Most important of all, don't punish or shame your child for having emotions; instead, teach them that there are both right and unacceptable ways to express them.

Prayer isn't going to teach your baby not to cry when mommy and daddy desperately need an hour of sleep, and it won't make your two-year-old stop a tantrum. From age three and up, you can start incorporating emotions into prayer, which will help your child identify their emotions and learn the correct ways to express or channel them. For example, a prayer said by the parent could be: "Dear God, please help Suzie when she is afraid. Let her be brave and not be scared of the dark anymore, because You will protect her. Amen." Older children can include their emotions and how they want to regulate them in their own prayers; for example, "Dear God, I'm sorry I yelled at my brother when I got angry. Please help me keep calm and be kind, even when I am upset. Amen."

Gratitude and Positivity

Children who develop a mindset geared toward gratitude and positivity will grow into adults who are appreciative rather than entitled and optimistic instead of despondent. Adults without a foundation of gratitude and positivity and who don't have prayer to turn to for solace may easily find themselves turning to unhealthy habits such as comfort eating, alcohol abuse, or extravagant shopping to distract themselves when their lives don't turn out as planned. Children without a grateful and positive mindset miss out on the healthy ability to accept things when they don't get their way. On a spiritual level, these children may grow up unable to accept that God's will is greater than their own, which paves the way for a lifetime of disappointment, resentment, and stress. A lack of gratitude also signifies a focus on the material, temporary world instead of a spiritual longing for an eternity in Heaven.

Did you know that scientists have studied the effects of thankfulness on physical and psychological health? Having a grateful attitude may help people sleep better, have a healthier cardiovascular system, and experience less inflammation (Jans-Beken et al., 2019).

The first step in teaching your children gratitude is to be a living example. Express gratitude in your everyday life, and your children will hear when and how it is appropriate to show thankfulness. Always include gratitude in your prayers to cement the concept in your children that God is the ultimate source of all good things and that people who do good things for others are fulfilling God's will.

To explain gratitude to children, you should try to use language that is appropriate for their age. Children might not yet be able to understand abstract gratitude, such as being grateful for existence or for being tested by God. Use everyday examples drawn from your child's experience to explain gratitude, such as having food, a comfortable, warm bed, good friends, pets, and a loving family. Encourage your children to tell God that they are grateful in their daily prayers.

Teach your children how to have a positive attitude by showing them through your words, actions, and prayers that you have faith in God's blessings. Read them the Bible and children's stories about people who kept a positive mindset in the face of adversity. Also, teach your children that prayer should be done in a spirit of trust that God will answer their prayers and send good things on their path.

Fears and Anxieties

Prayer can soothe anxiety and provide comfort when we are afraid. Remember that God created all of our emotions and declared His creation to be perfect. This means that there is nothing inherently wrong with experiencing fear or anxiety. God gave us fear to alert us to danger, and fear isn't less real or intense when the danger is something that can't really hurt us. When we are fearful, certain hormones flood our bodies, causing us to feel anxiety. Because we all have different minds and bodies, people experience anxiety and fear differently, with some people experiencing these emotions very strongly. Don't invalidate or belittle your children if they are fearful or anxious and you aren't, as their emotions can be overwhelmingly strong for them.

By putting our faith in God's protection, our fears and anxieties can be greatly relieved. This is where prayer is invaluable. When your children are fearful, remind them that they can talk to God about their worries and ask their all-powerful Father to comfort them. Help is just a prayer away!

In the next chapter, we'll examine Bible stories that are useful when teaching your children how to pray.

Chapter 6

BIBLICAL STORIES AND PRAYER

The Bible provides many examples of prayers for different purposes. In this chapter, we'll focus on how the Bible can help teach children how to pray. Your children will enjoy the stories, engage their imaginations with the illustrations in a children's Bible, and learn how God answered prayers in His own way according to His wisdom.

Lessons From Biblical Prayers

In this section, we'll look at some Biblical prayers and what they can teach us about our relationship with God. We'll discover that faith is more important than long, flashy prayers, that obedience to God's law will be rewarded, and that God can hear us without words, anywhere.

Faithfulness

In the time of Daniel, King Darius made a law that forbade anyone from praying to anyone but him for 30 days. Daniel remained faithful to God's commandment that believers should only worship God. Daniel knew he would get the death penalty if he didn't obey the king, but he remained dedicated to God and his prayer routine by praying three times a day. It wasn't long before Daniel was accused of breaking the law, and although the king loved Daniel and tried to save him, not even he could change a law once it was decreed. Daniel and three of his friends, who also prayed to God, were sentenced to be thrown into a lion's den.

The next day, Darius rushed to the lion's den and called out to Daniel in hopes that Daniel and his friends had survived against all odds. Daniel's faithfulness in prayer was indeed rewarded. He told Darius that God sent an angel to keep the lions' mouths closed.

Sincere Private Prayer

Hannah, the wife of the priest Elkanah, desperately wanted a child. One day, she prayed privately to God, with tears streaming down her face and only her lips moving. Eli, the high priest, saw this and thought Hannah was acting strangely because of too much wine. He chastised Hannah and told her to stop drinking. Hannah replied that she was telling God about her hurt and heartbreak. Eli then understood that Hannah was in sincere private prayer and hoped that God would answer her prayer. Nine months later, God blessed Hannah with her child, Samuel. You don't have to pray out loud for God to hear your prayers!

It is interesting that Hannah didn't tell Eli what she prayed for or why she was crying. She wanted to speak to God privately, and Eli didn't ask her what she said. Sometimes we want to share our sorrows only with God, and this privacy should be respected.

Unselfishness

Solomon was still very young when he took over the throne from his father, David. He knew he didn't have the knowledge to carry out the duties of a king and felt over-whelmed at the thought of governing God's chosen people. Instead of complaining to his advisors about being thrown into a difficult situation or deciding that ruling a kingdom was too much work, Solomon prayed for wisdom and discernment.

God was very pleased because it was an unselfish prayer. Solomon was now the head of state, and he could have asked to become a great and famous king, have unlimited riches, or achieve military victories. Instead, Solomon thought of the people of his kingdom and asked to be blessed with the qualities that would make him a good ruler capable of making the right choices. This unselfish prayer was rewarded with wisdom and discernment, and as extra blessings, God granted Solomon wealth, honor, and a long life.

Belief

A Roman centurion prayed with such unshakable belief in the power and authority of Jesus that Jesus remarked that the centurion's faith was stronger than that of any Israelite! The centurion's prayer was a simple request for Jesus to just say the word, and his servant would be healed. Faith was rewarded, and the servant, who was on his deathbed, was restored to health.

This Bible story teaches us that it isn't necessary to say long or complicated prayers or to include certain words. The centurion didn't say "amen" or "in Jesus' name"; he simply asked Jesus to heal his servant. In matters of the spirit, faith is much more important than words.

Persistence

Jesus explained the value of persistent prayer with a parable about a widow who kept pleading with a judge. The judge didn't care about people or God and was initially not bothered to give the widow justice in her case. However, the widow didn't give up and kept asking the judge until she wore him down, and he decided to grant her justice.

This parable doesn't mean that God only cares when we nag and pester. God isn't an uncaring or lazy judge! Instead, Jesus used this parable to show us that persistence can be a sign of faith. When we don't have our prayers answered immediately, we shouldn't stop asking but should have faith that God will provide.

Hope

Jonah prayed even when he was inside the whale's stomach! He gave us the example of clinging to God for hope against all odds. In his prayer, he accepted that his predicament was God's will, and he didn't get angry about it or give up hope. Jonah had so much hope that he included thanksgiving for his rescue in his prayer, even while still in the whale's belly. God answered the prayer by having the whale vomit Jonah out onto dry land.

The unshakable hope and trust that Jonah placed in God teach us that when we can't understand why God has put us in a certain situation, God knows what He's doing. Keep praying, and thank the Lord sincerely when He answers your prayers.

Surrender to God's Will

Jesus knew He was going to be crucified and suffer for the sins of billions of people on the cross. The knowledge of the agony to come made Him literally sweat blood. As the beloved son of God, Jesus only had to say the word, and God would have spared Him from the cross. Yet Jesus chose to surrender to God's will and submit to His greater plan.

He didn't ask God to change His plans, but He prayed that God would spare Him only if it was God's will. Jesus set us the example that we must accept God's will as greater than our own.

Bring Storytelling Into Prayer Time

Fairy tales, such as the old classic *Little Red Riding Hood*, hammer home the lesson to our children that talking to strangers (and wild animals) isn't a good idea. Although we tell our children what is safe and what should be avoided, they are curious by nature and need a little extra encouragement to pay heed to good advice, which is why we repeat the lessons in the form of stories. By using stories during prayer time, we bring spiritual truths to our children in a form they can easily understand and are more likely to pay attention to and remember.

If you can't make up stories, turn to the children's Bible or a storybook for age-appropriate narratives to help you illustrate abstract concepts.

Creating an Age-Appropriate Narrative

An age-appropriate narrative simply means making up a story around a spiritual concept in a way that it is relatable and interesting to a child. For example, your child isn't old enough to understand a dictionary definition of forgiveness but will understand it if you explain it through a story about one bird forgiving another for accidentally breaking its nest. Here are some tips that may help you create a narrative:

- Decide what concepts you want to explain through the story, such as faith, worship, trust, hope, and forgiveness.

- Make the characters of your narrative fun and child-friendly. Your children will respond better to a gnome in fairyland or a talking moose teaching them about friendship than a CEO giving a talk about team building.

- The setting of your story is important. It can be somewhere familiar, such as a house or school, or somewhere imaginary, such as a land far, far away. Avoid settings that children can't relate to, such as rush-hour traffic, board meetings, or the office.

- The concept you want to use in your story will be better understood if it is part of a child's experience. If you have more than one child, use siblings in your story. If your child has a favorite animal or color, make it part of the story. Using your child's name for one of the animal characters can also help capture your child's attention.

- Keep your language on your children's level. It is no use trying to explain repentance with words such as "remorse" to a preschooler. Instead, use words such as sorry, feeling bad, and unhappy.

- Children love hearing stories where the storyteller uses grand gestures and different voices. Embrace your inner actor and have some fun with the stories.

- Consider recording your stories for your children to watch when they are bored or need to revisit a specific concept. Your grandchildren and perhaps your great-grandchildren will treasure these recordings or videos, and they will become heirlooms to help guide them spiritually after you're gone.

- You can help the concept or lesson sink in by making the story interactive, such as by letting your children draw a picture and make up a short prayer related to the story.

Parallels Between Bible Stories and Children's Experiences

Thankfully, modern children don't have to face many of the challenges of biblical times, such as slavery, famine, and invading armies. Children can relate to other biblical stories, such as the following:

Noah built his ark even when everyone else told him he was wasting his time. His unwavering trust and obedience to God's commands allowed him and his family to survive the flood while saving the animals. The story is relatable to children because they also have to listen to and trust their parents like Noah trusted God. Also, they tend to love animals, which makes Noah's ark an opportunity to learn about different kinds of animals.

Children may struggle with jealousy and feelings of being overshadowed by their older, more accomplished siblings. The story of Joseph is relatable in families where there is natural sibling rivalry and occasional jealousy. (Fortunately, children can't sell annoying siblings into slavery anymore!) Joseph's siblings were consumed by jealousy when their father gave him a special colorful coat. Explain to your children that Jacob didn't love any of his children less than Joseph, but he had many children and only one special coat. The older children should have been mature enough to be happy for Joseph and not jealous, knowing that they also had received special favors when they were younger.

Joseph never gave up and always behaved according to God's will, and he eventually rose to prominence in Egypt. Ultimately, he was reconciled with his brothers, and they were all happy to be together again. Joseph forgave his brothers, and this was the key to their joyous reunion. The story of Joseph teaches children to let bygones be bygones and not hold grudges.

When David was still a young shepherd, he defeated the giant Goliath with only his faith and a sling. Children understand what it is like to be the small ones in a world of "giant" adults. They also want to be brave heroes just like David (yes, girls like to be heroes too). David's victory tells children that they can be small yet mighty if they have faith. They don't have to be the best at everything; just having faith and doing their best is enough in the eyes of God.

Small children will feel special and divinely loved when they hear the story of Jesus blessing the little children. With much of the Bible and church preaching often going over children's heads, it is easy for them to feel left out of spiritual matters. Knowing that Jesus singled children out for a special blessing will add to their confidence and self-worth.

Join me in the next chapter, where we'll discuss interactive prayer activities.

Chapter 7

INTERACTIVE PRAYER ACTIVITIES

Children, especially those who have grown up with mobile phones and computers, are used to being stimulated by bright colors, short snippets of information, and child-centered entertainment. Their minds have adapted to deal with media that older people may find chaotic. Because of this, children may find it challenging to quiet their minds long enough to properly focus on prayer and may even find it boring. Keep them engaged and interested in a deep spiritual life with interactive prayer activities. We've briefly mentioned some interactive activities in previous chapters, and this chapter will be dedicated solely to ideas on interactive prayer.

Arts and Crafts Related to Prayer

Prayer is an expression of the needs of the inner self, and children often enjoy expressing themselves through making things. Combine arts and crafts with prayer to add an extra dimension of meaning and expression to your children's spiritual routine.

Prayer Bracelets

Prayer bracelets come from the Eastern Orthodox Church, where believers have been wearing them since 1054 to guide and remind them of key concepts during prayer. Catholics are also familiar with the use of beads in the rosary, which they use to keep track of memorized prayers. The movement of the beads through the hands during prayer can also provide a familiar comfort and aid in focus.

Differently colored or shaped beads can represent concepts such as love, forgiveness, and gratitude. These bracelets are very helpful in teaching children to pray, as they can focus on the meaning of one or more beads when they talk to God. Wearing the bracelet throughout the day also serves as a reminder to live according to the values represented by the beads. Prayer bracelets can also help bring others to God; when they see the bracelet and ask about it, it opens up conversations about prayer and faith.

The colors of the prayer beads usually have these meanings:

- Blue represents being baptized with the Holy Spirit and/or with water.

- Green indicates spiritual growth.

- Black represents sin and the need for forgiveness.

- Red is a reminder of the blood of Jesus and our physical lives.

- White symbolizes repentance, cleansing of sins, holiness, and God's grace.

- Yellow or gold is associated with Heaven.

- Since ancient times, purple has been the color of royalty. As a prayer bead, purple stands for the kingdom of God.

You don't have to go the traditional route. If, for example, your child associates gold with Jesus, then use it in that context. Prayer is personal, and so are our color perceptions.

How to Make a Prayer Bracelet

The complexity of the beads depends on your child's age. Very young children will enjoy making a bracelet with about four brightly colored beads. The meaning of the beads should be simple, such as:

- Bead 1: Believe in God.

- Bead 2: Pray.

- Bead 3: Be kind.

- Bead 4: Do your best.

Having your child make a prayer bracelet can make prayer time more fun, but keep in mind that young fingers can slide beads better over thick string, pipe cleaners, paracord, or leather strips. Thin strings aren't suited for their still-developing hand-eye coordination, and they do best with larger beads. You may have to lend a hand and retie the knots when the children are done.

Older children might want to make a Lord's Prayer bracelet. They can arrange the beads in an order that they will be reminded of the words until they have learned the prayer by heart. For example, a yellow bead representing Heaven can be the prompt for "Our Father, Who art in Heaven." It is okay to use the same color more than once in a prayer bracelet, and your children can also mix and match different shapes and sizes of beads.

Prayer Painting

Children love expressing themselves through finger paints, watercolors, crayons, and colored pencils. The younger they are, the messier the expression, but it is the thought that counts, so be patient and let them do their artwork with a trash or shopping bag underneath the paper to spare your furniture.

One fun way of helping children develop thankfulness is by making a gratitude collage. The children can stick magazine cutouts, drawings, paintings, or photos of things they are grateful for onto a poster. The poster can then go up on a wall in the children's or family's prayer space.

Family Prayer Flags

The whole family can take part in a prayer flag project. Take an old sheet or large piece of white or light-colored linen, gather the family, and have everyone paint a representation in words or images of what prayer means to them. The flag doesn't have to be completely covered, leaving space for the family to add more later. The prayer flag can be spread out whenever someone needs a little extra spiritual inspiration. A prayer flag covered with things each family member is grateful for can become a special decoration at Thanksgiving. A family's prayer flag represents everyone's growth, hopes, loves, and fears, as well as their spiritual journey with God, and thus, it should be treasured and treated with respect.

Prayer Journals

A prayer journal is more than a diary in which you record what you prayed for. It is a collection of verses that speak to your heart, lists of things you're grateful for, inspired dreams, insights, reminders for prayer requests, hopes for the future, and thanks for prayers answered.

Children who aren't used to regular journaling may start a journal only to abandon it a few days later. Help them make journaling a part of their prayer routine by setting aside a few minutes every day after evening prayers for the whole family to write in their journals. Yes, that includes you, because children learn best by example.

Many journals end up looking more like overstuffed files that are full of loose papers, photos, letters, and even recipes for Thanksgiving desserts! Those are the best journals, as they reflect an active prayer life that testifies to God being present in all aspects of daily life.

Personal Illustrated Bible and Prayer Book

Children (and craft-loving adults) can make their own illustrated Bibles with their favorite stories, inspirational verses, and prayers. The easiest way to get started is with a hardcover store-bought schoolbook, preferably with alternating blank and lined pages, although an ordinary blank book will also work. Your child can write Bible stories and prayers in it and illustrate it with drawings or magazine cutouts. Older children might want to experiment with calligraphy and different paint techniques for their personal, self-written Bibles to resemble medieval illuminated manuscripts. Hint: Metallic craft paint is a good alternative to gold leaf and can have the same effect.

If you want to make an illustrated book of your children's favorite Bible stories for story time, you can delight your youngsters with a pop-up book. There are several tutorials online that can guide you through the process step-by-step, and it's surprisingly easy.

Prayer Jars

Imagine how comforting it will be to physically see the prayers that ask God to guide, help, and bless your family. A prayer jar helps you see these prayers, and all you need is an empty glass container, a pen, and some precut paper strips. Keep the prayer jar where everyone can see it, such as by the front door, in the kitchen, or on a mantelpiece. Anyone walking by the jar can write a short prayer and drop it in the jar. Thanksgiving is the ideal time to read all the paper strips and give thanks for all the answered prayers and blessings.

Join me in the next chapter, where we'll look at the difficult questions children are likely to ask about prayer and God.

Chapter 8

ANSWERING DIFFICULT QUESTIONS ABOUT PRAYER

It is inevitable that your children will have questions about prayer, and some of these questions can leave you tongue-tied if you are unprepared. In this chapter, we'll discuss some of the questions children are most likely to ask about prayer.

Unanswered Prayers

God doesn't answer prayers according to our wants; He answers them according to His greater plan. Sometimes, that greater plan means that God will say no or answer our prayers in ways we may not understand. God isn't a genie who just grants our wishes! He is the creator of the entire universe and has deep knowledge of things we can't begin to imagine, so we can trust that He knows what is best for us.

Your children might find it confusing that God is able to do anything yet may refuse to use His power on occasion. In their innocence, children may pray that God would let them fly or see through walls like a superhero and then wonder why God didn't give them these abilities. Because young children can't yet fully distinguish between trivial wishes and prayer, we can only smile at them and patiently explain that people would have no privacy if some could see through walls and birds would be frightened if they saw people flying.

Older children who pray about more serious issues, such as healing for a sick loved one, may become angry and disappointed if their prayers aren't answered. In such cases, remind them of the prayer of Jesus in the Garden of Gethsemane, where He asked God to let the bitter cup of crucifixion pass from Him, *if* it was His will. If God had answered Jesus' prayer, no one would be saved through His sacrifice. Sometimes, God lets our hearts break, or our bodies suffer, or our minds deteriorate. However, worldly suffering is temporary, while our reward is eternal. God's design has everything fitting together and working according to His plan for the greater good. We can be assured that in Heaven, God will dry our tears and wipe all suffering from our souls. Jesus didn't stop praying when God didn't answer His prayer; instead, He asked His disciples to pray with Him, and even when they fell asleep, He kept praying.

The Nature of Prayer Responses

Because of our limited understanding, we aren't always aware that God has answered our prayers. Here are some prayer responses that we might miss if we expect God to answer only in the way we expect Him to:

- God can answer with a "no." If He refuses to give us something, it is because what we have asked for would not be good for us or be part of God's grand design for the greater good. For example, a child might pray for a bicycle for Christmas. God might have other plans. This could be because God knows that buying a bike would put the parents in financial hardship, or because God knows an accident might occur in your street and a child with a bike would be severely injured that day. Ultimately, we can only guess why God says no, but since He knows everything and can see the future, we can put our trust in His wisdom.

- Sometimes, we must accept that God will grant us what we prayed for, but *not yet*. We should keep praying and trusting God even if we feel like giving up. God may answer us with a last-minute miracle or fulfill our prayers when we least expect it. We must remember that we are bound by time, but God, being eternal, knows the exact time when things should happen.

- Don't be surprised when God answers your prayer in *a way you weren't prepared for*. For example, if you ask God to make you an inspiration to others, He might put difficulties in your life so that you will inspire others by overcoming or learning to accept your hardships. Spiritual development isn't an easy road, but it is a rewarding one.

- God may answer your prayers by showering you with blessings, but *indirectly and discreetly*. God can be so subtle and gentle that we sometimes don't even notice His hand in our lives! Imagine a child asking God to help them earn extra money for their family in a time of need. Instead of giving the child a job as a driveway sweeper, God gives one of the parents an opportunity for a better-paying job. The family will have much better finances with this than with the meager income a child may bring. Besides, God knows that a child working as a sweeper might put them on the radar of wicked people.

Resilience

We know that God causes everything to work together for good. This doesn't mean that bad things that happen to us due to the choices of bad people are good! God's plan is directed toward a greater good that we can't yet comprehend. God's ability to know all things enables Him to use even bad things toward an ultimate defeat of evil. This can be compared to a chess grand master who allows some pieces to be captured to lure an opponent into a trap and ultimately win the game.

When God doesn't answer our prayers and allows bad things to happen, God isn't indifferent to our suffering. God is love, and love always cares deeply. Our Heavenly Father mourns with us, cries with us, and shares our anger at injustices, but He allows things to happen for a greater reason. When we accept that, we become spiritually resilient. Spiritual resilience is part of being spiritually mature, and it is the quality that makes us bounce back and keep fighting the good fight. Life will never keep you down if you trust in God's wisdom and love.

Keep Talking!

When prayers aren't answered right away, we should keep praying. God isn't an idol kept on a shelf to be dusted off only when we want something. Keep praying with the faith that God will answer your prayers in the way that He deems best. Pray to God every day, just as you would send texts, call, or visit your very best friend. When we only pray because we want something in the material world, we miss out on the true miracle of prayer—that we, as insignificant sinners, can have deep and loving conversations with the Creator of the universe!

When Your Children Are Disappointed in Prayer

Children live in the here and now, and this, coupled with their lack of experience, makes disappointment feel as if the world has come to an end. It is a big emotion for our young ones, and unfortunately, they can feel this crushing emotion when their prayers aren't answered. It can lead to doubts about the existence of God and anger at a God who allows bad things to happen. Here are some ideas to help you guide your children through disappointment:

- **Acknowledge your child's feelings.** To you, it might not be a big deal that your child wasn't chosen for a team or asked to a party, but your child's world is much smaller than yours, and they may have pinned all their hopes, dreams, and prayers on a specific outcome.

- **Explain to your child that when God says no, it is because He has something different planned that will work toward ultimate good.** We can only see and understand a tiny part of the whole picture. God has a purpose for everything, even unanswered prayers.

- **Comfort your child and let them know that it is okay to grieve and feel disappointment and that the awful feeling will pass.** Don't make fun of them or belittle them for having hurt feelings, or they may start hiding their emotions and resenting you.

- **Encourage your child to keep trying or to modify their dreams.** If your child didn't get good grades after studying hard, a tutor or an online tutorial may be a good idea. Think of ways to help your child reach their ideals, but be realistic. An unathletic child might not be chosen for a sports team, but there are other activities where the child may excel.

- **The most important action you can take is to set an example.** Show your children that you trust God, and keep praying! Pray with your child after a disappointment, and when you experience a disappointment yourself, let your family pray with you. Let your family see that you practice what you preach when you say you have faith in God.

Doubts About Prayers

In this section, we look at ways to address children's doubts and skepticism about prayer. Very young children, who accept the powers of Superman, find it easy to believe in God's unlimited power. No wonder Jesus told us to be like little children; He wanted us to have their unshakable trust and faith. Let's explore how we can instill and maintain this childlike faith in our older children.

Open Communication

If you don't allow children to ask questions about God and prayer, they might lose their faith and cover it up by saying what they think you want to hear. Let your children express their doubts and skepticism without fear of judgment or ridicule. When communication is open and honest, your children will take you into their confidence and turn to you for help and guidance. Here are some guidelines for open communication with your doubting child:

- Give your child undivided attention while they talk to you about spiritual matters, including their doubts. If you show genuine interest and do your best to answer their questions, your child will be more comfortable to open up and share their thoughts.

- There is a difference between preaching and having a conversation. Your doubting child wants a conversation where they are free to ask questions and talk about their point of view. Giving your child a lecture and chastising them for doubting won't address their doubts, and both of you will be stuck on square one.

- Your conversation should be age-appropriate. Answers that go over your child's head or underestimate their intelligence will not address their doubts and may make your child hesitant to take you into their confidence in the future.

Seeking Understanding

Some children never question the existence of God or the power of prayer and will keep their faith strong all of their days. But what happens when you have a child who questions everything and is a natural skeptic?

Here are some tips to help you address your children's doubts with empathy and understanding:

- Realize your child's soul isn't lost because they are skeptical. It is a sign of high intelligence and a beautiful curiosity about life if your child doesn't accept everything at face value. Jesus didn't hate Thomas for doubting His identity but instead invited His disciple to touch His wounds to be sure it really was Him!

- Be open to your child's questions and criticisms of the Bible. If you need help addressing their doubts, you can read an apologetics book with your child. Apologetics is a religious field that means defending beliefs. There are apologetics books and videos available for all ages.

- You can't force someone to believe. If your child can't believe in God despite having their questions answered, accept it and keep praying that God will change your child's heart. Don't resent your child or treat them differently; after all, everything is part of God's grand design. Keep living in faith to set an example for your child of how good and fulfilling a relationship with God can be. It is natural for children to go through a stage where they believe everything their parents tell them is wrong, and it is equally natural for mature adults to realize their elders had it right all along!

Encouraging Critical Thinking

It is good to have faith, but we can't trust every source. There is much intentional and unintentional deception in the world and so much conflicting information that finding real facts has become an art form. This is where critical thinking is invaluable. Critical thinking is when we analyze and evaluate information to find solutions to problems, make decisions that will result in good outcomes, and set realistic, attainable goals.

Critical thinking isn't the enemy of faith. Many of the world's best thinkers were firm believers in God, such as Isaac Newton, Albert Einstein, and Galileo Galilei. They used their faith in the Creator as an inspiration to explore His creation.

Being able to think critically gives your child the lifelong advantage of good decision-making and problem-solving skills. Let's explore a few methods that you can use to encourage and develop your children's critical thinking abilities:

- Set an example by researching statements heard on the news or on social media to find out if they are true. Involve your children in the research by asking them to help you verify the facts. Your children will feel valued when you trust their research skills, and this will encourage them to do independent fact-finding.

- Games that involve strategy and foresight stimulate the mind to sift through and evaluate information. Play board games with your child instead of watching TV, or have a short riddle competition after dinner.

- Develop their problem-solving skills by challenging them with a problem scenario and asking them to come up with three solutions. For example, ask your children to indicate "five" without using numbers or words or move an object without using their hands.

- Wire puzzles and Rubik's cubes will strongly challenge your children's problem-solving abilities and develop patience at the same time. These puzzles also make inexpensive, durable, and fun gifts.

- Allow your children to make choices (within reason) and give them an age-appropriate allowance to teach them the real-life consequences of their decisions. Children learn quickly how to make responsible choices when they figure out that they can afford either one movie or ten ice creams!

Sharing Personal Experience

Share your own struggles with faith and skepticism. Telling your child about the times when you doubted and what changed your mind gives your child something they can relate to. This can encourage your child to communicate openly because they will see that you have been there too.

You don't have to share your own journey immediately when your child tells you about their doubts. If you make the conversation all about you, your child might feel as if you haven't truly listened. So, take some time and do a little preparation beforehand. Here are a few tips to help you share your experience in the most effective way:

- Prepare for the conversation by thinking exactly what you want to share. Don't share an issue that causes you doubt if it might violate anyone's privacy or if the issue isn't age-appropriate.

- Decide on a time and place to talk with your child that will be free of distractions and interruptions. The conversation might end up longer than you initially planned if your child has several questions.

- Before jumping in with your story, acknowledge your child's doubts and skepticism, and thank them for trusting you enough to be honest about their struggles.

- Talk about your journey through doubt and the effect it had on your faith. Mention the questions you wrestled with and how you found answers.

- If your questions weren't answered but you decided to trust in God to reveal the truth to you when He thinks you are ready, tell this to your child as well. Unanswered questions are part of life, and although they can be wondered about, obsessing over them is unhealthy.

- Explain to your child that having doubts ultimately led you to a stronger faith and deeper understanding of spiritual matters.

- Answer any questions your child may have regarding your journey and be honest. If your own doubts were never resolved and your questions still await answers, tell your child that this is the case. Your child may take heart from seeing you being faithful to God despite having doubts.

- End the conversation by reassuring your child that you are always available to help them as best you can and that you are happy to pray with them about their doubts if they would want.

Balancing Faith and Logic

Prayer straddles two worlds: the material where we are and the spiritual where we want to be. Faith and logic combine to form a bridge between these worlds, which can easily be crossed by both the analytical mind and the ethereal soul.

Exploring the Intersection Between Faith and Reason

Faith needs to rest on a sensible foundation; otherwise, it is folly. We base our faith in God on His words and deeds. Because we conclude that the complexity of the universe necessitates a Creator, we trust that the Creator knows what He is doing and is powerful enough to accomplish anything He wants. When the Almighty Creator tells us that He loves us and wants us with Him in Heaven forever, we have faith because we trust His character and power that He reveals to us in the Bible, in prayer, and in the world around us.

Reason tells us that we need evidence for our beliefs. We don't pray to Superman, despite his superpowers and ability to help people. Reason keeps us from putting our trust in a fictional character who has no power in real life. When we read about God causing a worldwide flood, reason enables us to realize that such a flood is possible and that there is archaeological and geological evidence that supports its occurring. Thus, reason is the foundation that tells us God is possible and real.

When our faith intersects with reason, a great awakening occurs in our being. Our faith increases to the point of being unshakable because we know we believe in the truth. Our reason expands to a deeper understanding of spiritual matters because we have faith that helps us focus on what is truly important.

Your child doesn't have to base their prayer experience on blind faith. Adding reason, research, and discussion to their spiritual journey will enhance and deepen their relationship with God and help resolve their doubts and skepticism.

Encouraging Exploration of Faith and Reason

Children love the adventure and excitement of discovering something new. Encouraging them to explore the complexities and nuances of logic and faith helps them develop a balance between mind and soul.

Value your children's innate curiosity and let them know that it is okay to question everything. Provide them with books and videos that discuss faith from different points of view. Older children can read books that try to discredit faith and then write their own counterarguments, which they can store in their prayer journals or read to other members of their prayer group or Sunday school.

Watch documentaries with your children that discuss the civilizations of biblical times. This will deepen their understanding of the cultures and mythologies of peoples mentioned in the Bible. Knowing how people experienced the world in ancient times will open up fresh points of view for your children when they read Bible stories.

Leveraging Symbolism and Metaphor

Symbols and metaphors connect the abstract with the concrete to make concepts easier to understand. You can explain abstract concepts to your child with the help of these tips:

- Make a list of the abstract concepts you want to explain to your child. Examples of abstract concepts related to prayer include belief, trust, grace, forgiveness, guidance, love, hope, and salvation.

- When deciding which symbols and metaphors to use, take your child's experiences and personality into account. For example, if you want to use a symbol to represent spiritual guidance, a compass would be suitable for a child who loves the outdoors or is a scout. Alternatively, your child's interests might make a lighthouse or a guide dog a more relatable symbol.

- Explain to your child how the symbol represents a concept. Most children are already familiar with a heart as a symbol of love and two hands together as indicating prayer.

- Children may respond better to a metaphor used in a story than simply making a comparison. Instead of saying "the fruits of the Spirit," you can tell a story about a beautiful tree in Heaven whose fruits are named after good qualities such as love and kindness.

- Biblical parables are easily understood, and if you use a children's Bible, the language will already be age-appropriate.

Teaching the Value of Mystery

A mystery is intriguing and invites us to investigate, but some mysteries remain unexplained. The same is true for some aspects of spirituality. Since we don't live in the spiritual realm and fall far short of God's unlimited understanding, we have to accept that some things will always be unknowable.

We know that living things breathe, feed, and grow. Science can explain how we breathe, what happens inside our bodies when we eat, and how cells get bigger. But we can't explain why things are alive, and not even the best scientist can create life from scratch. Creation and life are mysteries that we can't solve, but contemplating them can help us better appreciate the greatness of God.

Take your children outside on a clear, warm evening and let them simply gaze at the stars. Remind them that God created each of these suns and planets that are so far away that they appear as mere pinpricks of light to us. What love God has for us, to create entire worlds to be lights for us at night! Of all spiritual mysteries, the greatest is how deeply God loves us.

When pondering the mysteries of God with your children, celebrate the acceptance of His unknowable grace and power with prayer and worship. The hymn *How Great Thou Art* is ideal for a musical family to express the awe they feel when pondering God's mysteries and the glories of His creation.

Using Analogies and Stories

To illustrate the power of *faith*, you can tell your children how elite athletes are encouraged to believe that they'll win as part of their training. Explain to your child that even a tiny bit of true faith can accomplish great things because faith gives us a winning mindset and keeps us in touch with the all-powerful God. Also, just as a little seed grows into a large tree if the gardener regularly waters it, faith also needs to be tended through prayer in order for it to grow.

God is everywhere, even though we can't see Him. Your young child may understand His *omnipresence* better if you tell them that God is like air. Air is all around us, from the ground up into the sky. We can't see the air, but we know it is there because we can breathe it. Older children, especially those with an interest in science, may relate more to the presence of radio waves as an explanation of God being physically present but *invisible*. A radio can pick up a station without the radio waves being seen; thus, unseen doesn't mean absent!

When we unintentionally do something wrong, it is like spilling juice on our clothes. We are embarrassed, and everyone can see that we were careless. Fortunately, we can put our clothes in the wash, and the juice will rinse out. *Forgiveness* works the same way. God washes our guilt away and looks at us as if we are brand new again. Once we've been forgiven, God never thinks of our mistakes again.

In the next chapter, we'll explore faith traditions and how they are part of prayer.

Chapter 9

CONNECTING PRAYER TO FAITH TRADITIONS

In this chapter, we'll explore the role of prayer in different religions and how prayer traditions vary across cultures. Your child can develop an appreciation for the traditions of other people and discover that prayer is a universal feature of believing in a higher power. The knowledge of different prayer traditions can enrich a child's understanding of spiritual concepts and deepen their connection to the divine.

Learning About Prayer in Different Religions

Different religions have different beliefs about prayer and different ways of contacting their god or gods. Having a basic knowledge of other religions' spiritual practices can broaden your children's perspective on spirituality and help foster respect for the points of view of other faiths.

Comparative Analysis

In this section, we'll compare the differences and similarities of some other religions' prayer traditions.

Christianity

Christians use prayer to communicate directly with God, and it is acceptable at any time, whether in private or in groups. Traditionally, praying Christians fold their hands together, close their eyes, and bow their heads to keep their focus only on the prayer and to show humility and reverence to God. Prayers can be of any length, spur-of-the-moment, read from text, or memorized. No form of prayer is considered superior as long as it is sincere and not to get public admiration for the person praying.

Judaism

Although Jews can pray at any time, they also have specific prayers to be said at particular times, actions, religious festivals, and on the Sabbath. Prayer usually includes praise and thanksgiving. During prayer, Jews may close their eyes when certain phrases are said, and it is also customary to rock back and forth. Jews are expected to recite a specific prayer called the Shema twice daily. Orthodox Jewish men, when worshipping, reading scripture, or praying, cover their heads with a prayer shawl or a small cap to show humility. Two leather boxes strapped to the arm and forehead are also worn during morning prayer services. Many ultra-Orthodox men also wear a special belt made of cloth during prayer.

Islam

In Islam, prayer has certain rules. Muslims are required to pray five times daily, and when they pray, they must face the Kaaba. The Kaaba is a cubical building in Mecca that contains the Black Stone, which Muslims believe was given to Adam by God. The five prayers, said at specific times, follow a fixed structure that begins with a cleansing ritual. During the prayers, Muslims follow a special sequence of standing, bowing, prostrating (kneeling and touching the ground with their foreheads), and sitting, which they repeat while reciting verses from their scriptures. Muslims can pray alone, but they place great value in praying together as a community, especially on Fridays.

Hinduism

Hinduism has many gods, and believers choose certain gods for special devotion. How a Hindu prays depends on the traditional worship practices associated with a specific god. Some prayers are accompanied by floral or food offerings or incense. Prayer is usually in the form of mantras, which are repetitions of certain phrases. Believers can visit temples to pray as they please without having to attend a formal service.

Buddhism

Buddhists consider their belief system to be more of a philosophy and lifestyle than religion. Instead of praying to communicate with a divinity, Buddhists meditate to attain a mindset focused on achieving spiritual enlightenment, which they believe will free them from reincarnation and earthly suffering. To help them keep count of their 108 mantras, many Buddhists use prayer beads.

Respecting Differences

Learning about the prayer traditions of different cultures and religions can help your children understand that the yearning for something greater than ourselves is universal. Your children don't have to sacrifice or dilute their own beliefs to respect the traditions of others. It is also possible to take elements from other traditions to enhance their own prayer experience. The same way that eating Chinese food won't make you ethnically Chinese, placing flowers at your prayer area won't make you a Hindu. Perhaps a child who has difficulty blocking out distractions may focus better on prayer if they cover their head with a prayer shawl.

Sharing Stories of Faith

When families, prayer groups, or individuals share their personal stories of faith, children are exposed to firsthand testimony of the power and meaning of prayer.

Family Heritage

"Where do I come from?" is probably the first existential question any child asks. We like to feel connected with those who came before us and to be part of a lineage that stretches back to the beginning of creation. Our family heritage provides us with our physical features and, to a great extent, also with our spiritual practices. We tend to pray in the way our parents taught us, and our parents learned from our grandparents. We feel the power of a strong tradition when we, in turn, teach our own children the prayers that comforted our ancestors.

The family bond is strengthened when children hear personal stories of family members' faith. They can relate to stories such as how Great-Grandpa prayed for a job when he came back from serving in World War II or how Aunt Jane had faith that God would heal Uncle Jack's cancer. Your children know these people; even if they died before they were born, they still form part of the family's identity and traditions.

Personal Testimonies

Hearing someone share their personal experience of faith can be more inspirational and relatable than a generalized story. The spiritual becomes more concrete and understandable when children hear and see the effects of prayer and faith in real life.

Children need role models to emulate, and what better example for them to follow than a fellow believer who encourages them to pray though personal testimony! It is inspiring to hear the stories of people who overcame obstacles through their trust in God.

Furthermore, personal testimonies show us that God actively plays a part in the lives of everyday people. Their lived experience reflects the faithfulness of God in working all things toward a greater good. The testimonies help children understand that God answers prayers in ways that can sometimes be quite unexpected!

Cultivating Belief

A benefit of sharing personal stories of faith is that your children will have examples to reference if they find themselves in similar situations. They will have real-life templates to inspire them and help them overcome spiritual challenges. Having proof of the outcomes of faith helps children see that belief can have tangible, real effects.

Personal testimonies often involve miracles, the power of prayer, or the rewards of faithfulness, which can comfort children when they have doubts or are facing difficulties.

Your Child's Testimony

Your child has their own story of faith to share. Age isn't a barrier to faith, and many of your child's peers may be inspired by their testimony. As your child ages, they might like to look back at how they experienced faith as an innocent child and how their personal faith journey has progressed. For this reason, it is a good idea to record your child's testimony in a journal or as a video or audio recording.

Encourage and help your child formulate their own personal testimony. Here are some ways your child can share their testimony:

- Shy children or those with speech impediments may prefer to draw a picture to express how their faith has been rewarded.

- Youngsters with a flair for the dramatic might spice up their testimony through role-playing or performing a skit with some friends.

- Children who enjoy writing can write their testimony in a prayer journal, and if they are comfortable sharing, they can invite other believing friends over to read each other's testimonies.

- Thanks to the recording capabilities of smart phones, making a video or audio recording doesn't require specialized equipment or spending lots of money. An older child or a parent can record the testimony and store it safely on a flash drive, which can be kept privately or shared in a prayer group or during family prayer time.

Exploring Traditional Prayers From Your Own Faith

Some evergreen prayers touch our hearts as much as when they were first written, such as the interdenominational *Lord's Prayer* and, for Catholics, the *Hail Mary*. Discovering prayers from your own faith heritage deepens the sense of connection and community that helps keep our spiritual identities firmly rooted through the ages.

Cultural Roots

Different cultures have methods of connecting with the divine that may seem strange to us at first, but they can often be adapted to fit our own spiritual practices. For example, using dance as part of prayer may appeal to children with musical talents.

Let's explore some historical and cultural roots of traditional prayers:

- Some Christian denominations use prayer books containing prayers that can be recited privately or in church. The experience of sharing the same prayer as the other congregants promotes a powerful sense of community and belonging.

- The Eastern Orthodox Christian church follows ancient traditions that include the use of incense and icons to invite believers to foster a reverent atmosphere and promote focus on the spiritual realm. Eastern Orthodox believers use a prayer rope to aid them in repeating a short prayer called the *Jesus Prayer*. This prayer focuses on Jesus' name, and the many repetitions help people become aware of the presence of God.

- The Maori Christians of New Zealand draw on their indigenous culture when they pray. They enhance their prayer experience by performing a traditional dance called the Haka to symbolize strength and unity. To show gratitude for God's love and blessings, they also make food and flower offerings.

- Australian Aboriginal tribes connect with their spirit realm, which they call the Dreamtime, through stories and prayers. Before visiting the Dreamtime, they ritually purify their prayer space with smoke and paint special symbols on themselves.

- The Navajo Native American tribe uses traditional songs, chants, and sand paintings in their prayers.

- African Christians' traditions vary widely according to the diverse cultures and tribes, but most of them include dance and music to celebrate God's presence. Some cultures also incorporate traditional drumming and anointing with oil into their prayers.

- Asian Christians use age-old cultural spiritual practices such as incense, bowing, and chanting in their prayer practices.

- Christians in Jerusalem take part in a daily prayer outside a sanctuary where a priest makes an incense offering at the altar.

- The prayer wheel, originally a Tibetan Buddhist prayer tradition, is showing up in some Western Christian congregations, where people spin the prayer wheel to symbolize never-ending prayer to God. Christian prayer wheels contain Bible verses instead of Buddhist mantras. Critics of prayer wheels are concerned that they might devolve into a mindless action of spinning the wheel instead of sincere prayer.

Generational Continuity

Amazing Grace was written in 1779, and *How Great Thou Art* in 1885. These hymns were sung as worshipful prayers by our forefathers and are still part of many church services. What a blessing it is to connect with God by lifting our voices in these hymns, with the echoes of our ancestors adding their prayers!

Generational continuity of prayers, whether in the form of traditional hymns or mealtime blessings, allows us to become part of something timeless. Teaching your children these prayers, just as your parents learned them from their parents, fosters a sense of continuity, community, and heritage.

Sacred Reverence

The rich legacy of traditional prayer fosters reverence and respect for the faith of those who have gone before us. It connects us with the beliefs and practices of those who overcame life's struggles with only a Bible and a prayer, representing the hopes, faith, challenges, and dreams of our families and communities.

Most worship services have a certain structure and order. These rituals may include reciting the Apostles' Creed at the end of the service or singing a hymn after the homily. The structure adds a sense of familiarity and comfort, which grows into a spiritual reverence for the texts, hymns, and prayers of our tradition.

In olden times, all Christian services were conducted in Latin. Today, only a few Catholic congregations still use this ancient language. Having services in the language of the area makes the scriptures and rituals more accessible to everyone. However, some people who grew up with Latin services miss the sense of sacredness and history that isn't quite the same in modern versions.

The role of hymns shouldn't be underestimated in a service. Timeless melodies and traditional harmonies make us feel the reverence and awe that our prayers express. Music speaks to our hearts and lifts our prayers to the throne of God.

Personal Devotion

Traditional prayers and hymns are of no use if we don't make them part of our personal faith journey. A beautiful hymn sung in a glorious cathedral can inspire your child and make them feel connected to the tradition and community, but at the end of the day, it is your child's personal connection to God that is the most important for spiritual growth.

Teach your children the old prayers and songs and let them use them in their private prayer time. In times when they simply don't have the words to express their feelings to God, the old prayers will speak for them.

One day, when your children have grown old and the prayer journey of their youth is only a faded memory, they will hold the hands of your grandchildren, lift their faces to the stars, and sing *How Great Thou Art*.

In the next chapter, we'll look at strategies to encourage consistency in your children's prayer habits.

Chapter 10

ENCOURAGING PERSISTENCE IN PRAYER

Just like our bodies need daily nourishment, our spirits need the daily bread of prayer. Consistent, dedicated prayer should be as much part of your children's routine as showering and doing their homework. This chapter focuses on practical ways to encourage persistent prayer.

Establishing Prayer Goals

When children have a clear goal to aim for, it becomes easier for them to understand what it takes to reach that goal. Having prayer goals encourages the youngsters (and their parents, who may have started to rest on their laurels) to put in the work and do so consistently.

Learning how to set goals will not only help your children be dedicated to prayer but will also empower them to properly plan for anything they set their minds to. Clear goal setting can also boost your children's grades and improve their performance in extracurricular activities, and as adults, enable them to plan their career paths and work out sensible budgets.

Children from around age seven onwards are capable of the abstract thinking needed to set goals. Younger children can be encouraged to reach the goals you set them by writing the goal, such as "Pray before bedtime," on a poster and sticking a gold star next to it every day. Rewards will give them extra incentive, so remember to give them a small treat when they have a certain number of gold stars.

Clarifying Intentions

Vague goals are unattainable because you can't measure progress and success. A nebulous "I want to be successful at prayer" isn't specific enough to be a valid goal. "I want to pray at least twice a day with my full focus on God" is something that can be worked toward, and it is easy to check progress. Clarifying intentions is the first step in setting an attainable goal.

Any goal becomes easier once the intention is as specific as possible. For instance, "getting better grades" doesn't help your child start on the path toward better grades; it is just a vague dream with no way to plan how to get there. A better goal would be "Spend an extra half hour every day studying the math examples we did in class."

Setting Realistic Objectives

There are many inspirational stories of miracles or last-minute interventions through the power of prayer. It is important to explain to your children that miracles can and do happen, but it is more realistic to plan ahead as if a miracle won't happen. Miracles are extraordinary by nature, and God lets them happen only rarely. Have faith that God will listen to and answer your prayers, but be willing to put in effort from your side as well. After all, God gave us common sense and intelligence for a reason!

Gigantic goals can be achieved, but unless progress is planned in bite-sized, achievable chunks, it is very unlikely to come true. Many teenagers dream of becoming a music star, but unless they set achievable, realistic goals—such as working to save money for a musical instrument and taking music lessons—they don't have a workable plan to follow. The same principle applies to prayer goals. A goal to pray for an hour before bedtime is unrealistic. Children work hard at school, and they are still growing, which makes them simply too exhausted to focus for long when their brains are already flooded with sleep hormones. It will be more realistic to aim for two minutes of prayer at different times during the day.

Remember to add little rewards for achieving milestones. The rewards should match the achievement; otherwise, your children may become savvy and set goals that are too small in order to get frequent rewards. For example, a goal of saying "Amen" after each prayer and expecting a reward when they have done so for a week isn't realistic goal setting; it is manipulation!

Encouraging Reflection

Looking back lets us see how far we've come. Achieving a small goal gives us the advantage of experience. Knowing what you did right and what to avoid in the future makes it easier to set the next goal. It also boosts children's self-esteem and self-confidence when they review their achievements and remember the hard work they put in to make them happen.

Here are some ways reflecting on their prayer life can help your children set achievable goals:

- Your children will notice that some prayers are more likely to be answered in the way they expected. This helps them understand that God is more likely to help them achieve realistic goals than to fulfill wishful thinking. For example, your children may notice that God was truly with them during exams and that He answered their prayers for help to keep their minds calm and clear but didn't answer their prayers to give them full marks on tests they didn't study for. Once children understand that they have to put in effort to reach their dreams, their goals will be more realistic.

- Sometimes, God doesn't answer immediately but makes us wait until He decides the time is right. Your children will see that some of their past prayers were answered in God's time and that even though they might have felt like giving up, their perseverance was rewarded. This firsthand experience of the value of perseverance will help your children be patient when they set goals and not expect instant results.

- There are prayers that are too unrealistic to be answered. For example, if we pray for absolute peace with no one in the world having even a mild disagreement, it implies we expect God to interfere with the free will of everyone on earth. Scripture and experience tell us that God allows free will and will ask, but not force, people to act in certain ways. It is a waste of energy and ignores the nature of God to pray for unachievable goals. Your children might be surprised at how many times they have prayed for something that didn't line up with God's will. Both spiritual and material goals have to take into account that other people aren't accessories but have the God-given right to their own free will.

- Answered prayers teach us gratitude, and your children will understand that goals achieved are something to be grateful for. It is a privilege to have the opportunity to realize goals, and it is a blessing to have the ability to make our dreams a reality. When a goal is achieved, encourage your children to include God in their celebration.

Tracking Prayer Habits

Habits are so automatic that we seldom pay them any attention and thus miss out on what they can teach us. Prayer habits teach us to be disciplined and consistent in our walk with God. In this section, we'll discover how monitoring prayer habits cements self-discipline and accountability in your children. Here are some ways in which tracking prayer habits contributes to your child's spiritual and personal growth:

- Regularly reviewing prayer journals or other methods

of keeping track of prayer helps children stay on track with their daily prayer.

- Evaluating their prayer habits makes children responsible for their spiritual practices. Just as they are responsible for getting dressed and doing chores, they are responsible for their conversations with God.

- When your child looks back with a sense of accomplishment at their prayer habits, they will be motivated to stay dedicated to their spiritual routine.

- Monitoring the times when they stray from their prayer habits helps children identify stumbling blocks. For example, they might notice that they tend to neglect prayer on Saturday mornings because they rush out of bed to watch cartoons. This can easily be remedied by getting up only five minutes earlier or setting themselves a goal to pray first and then watch TV.

Parental Involvement

What can you do to help your children track their prayer habits?

Your children are more likely to stick to their prayer habits and keep track of their prayers through journaling or charts if you set regular prayer times for them. They will soon become used to praying at specific times and journaling directly afterward.

If you notice that your children never skip prayer time but they don't journal their prayers, you might encourage them to record their prayer experiences and goals in other ways. They can use charts, audiovisual recordings, or apps to help them track their prayer times and content.

Set an example by maintaining your own prayer habits, which include fixed prayer times and journaling.

Pay attention to your children's prayers. When one of their prayers is answered or they show growth in spiritual maturity, encourage them to praise God and thank Him in prayer for His blessings. Sometimes, your children might not notice these blessings, so you can draw their attention to them and remind them to write them down in their prayer journals.

Praise and encouragement will make your children feel they are on the right track and inspire them to maintain their prayer habits.

Recognizing Progress and Milestones

It can be hard to do something every day without anyone seeing your progress or offering a word of encouragement. A kind word of praise and a small celebration now and then lets your children know you notice and appreciate their efforts. Few things bring back enthusiasm like a pat on the back!

Acknowledging Efforts

Imagine you've been going to the office early every day for a month to do extra, unpaid work, such as washing everyone's mugs and checking that every pen writes smoothly. You don't have to do the extra work, and many people might think you are wasting your time, but it is important to you. Wouldn't you feel appreciated and motivated to continue if the boss called you into their office to give you a surprise bonus and tell your colleagues that you are faithful in the small things? Now, imagine you are a child who prays faithfully while their friends make fun of them and tell them they are wasting their time talking to an invisible Being. Just like you, children also need encouragement and praise and someone to acknowledge their efforts. Notice them praying, praise them for their dedication, and surprise them occasionally with a small gift or treat. Let them know you are proud of them and their accomplishments.

Milestone Rewards

It isn't necessary to make a big fuss over every small goal reached, but they still need to be acknowledged, even if only with an announcement at the dinner table or a small gift. Larger goals, which are definitive milestones on the road to achievement, deserve rewards that will encourage your children to stick to their plans and remain dedicated to reaching their goals. Here are some ideas for rewards that will motivate your children without breaking the bank:

- The first idea is what not to give your children. Candy as a reward can lead to dietary issues later in life if your child makes a subconscious connection between reward and sugar.

- Discount coupons are practical small gifts for children who get an allowance. If your children are required to buy their personal items with their allowance money, give them several coupons for their favorite products. Older children might appreciate coupons for popcorn and a movie ticket.

- Young children can be rewarded with you reading them an extra story at bedtime.

- Very young children will be delighted to receive bubbles.

- Big milestones can earn a child a day or two free from doing chores.

- If your family has a movie night or watches a TV show together, your child can pick the movie or show.

- Small children may be allowed to build a blanket fort in the living room and have it stay up for the weekend.

- Older children who achieve goals that prove their responsibility and maturity may be allowed to stay home alone or babysit as a reward.

- Giant milestones that took a lot of effort and time can be rewarded with a family outing to a restaurant, park, or sports game.

- You can give your children a little spending money and take them to a toy or craft shop.

- Gift cards that match your children's interests make sure they get a reward that they'll be excited about. These cards can be for books, clothes, sports gear, or a hobby shop.

- Other small gifts include sidewalk chalk, face paint, art supplies, themed pillowcases, a pajama day, or a family visit to the zoo or aquarium.

Community Recognition

We involve the community in our children's spiritual lives by having family prayer time, participating in prayer groups, and being members of a congregation. Being part of a like-minded group fosters a sense of belonging and encourages people to work toward common goals, such as fundraising for a new church roof. Our communities can provide comfort and support, as well as recognition that makes our children feel valued and special.

To involve your church or prayer group in your children's spiritual milestones, ask your pastor, priest, or reverend to congratulate your child when they reach a prayer goal. If your child reaches a major milestone, you might consider asking the worship leader or choir if they would sing your child's favorite hymn and dedicate it to your child as an acknowledgement of their goal achieved.

Dealing With Setbacks

There will probably be times in your child's life when they are overcome with doubts and discouragement. They might want to give up on prayer and rebel against family prayer. Instead of letting your child admit defeat and let go of their relationship with God, offer some guidance to help them overcome these spiritual challenges.

Encouraging Open Communication

Some children are naturally more inclined to talk about their problems, doubts, and fears. Others may need a little extra encouragement to open up. Here are a few ideas to open the lines of communication and avoid the dreaded monosyllabic response:

- Don't interrogate your child the moment they open the door. If they feel overwhelmed with questions when all they really want to do is put down their books and have a sandwich, they might answer all questions with an "okay" to end the conversation as quickly as possible.

- Greet your children with a loving, enthusiastic tone and give them time to settle down before asking them about school or their thoughts.

- If your child fears that you will judge or punish them harshly, they are more likely to keep quiet or lie rather than confide in you. Children are also more likely to avoid conversation if they have a parent prone to violent or verbally abusive outbursts, melting into tears, jumping to conclusions, or who has a track record of gossiping.

- It is fine to be happy and enthusiastic about your child's achievements, but if you overreact in such a way that your child feels embarrassed, your child might not share their triumphs with you next time.

- Imagine wrestling with an issue of faith, making an appointment with your pastor, and looking forward to getting counseling from someone you trust. How will you react if your pastor has one eye on his mobile phone or TV while you are pouring your heart out? Chances are, you will leave feeling frustrated, dismissed, and determined to never speak to your pastor about your faith again. The same is true for your child. Give your child your undivided attention during personal conversations and listen actively. Your child will be able to tell if your thoughts are elsewhere.

- Don't pry. A child who feels comfortable talking to you will do so when they are ready. Teenagers are especially put off when a parent keeps pushing them to discuss private matters. Unless your child is showing signs of being bullied, sexually abused, sexually active, displaying violent behavior, possibly using alcohol or drugs, planning to break the law, or developing a mental illness such as depression, there is no need to push. If your child does exhibit a red flag behavior, you should have a serious conversation about it, but only after you've consulted a professional for guidance on the most effective response and action.

- Ask your child questions that they have to answer with full sentences, not only a yes, no, or grunt. Instead of asking them if their day was good, ask them what interesting things they learned at school today. Pay enough attention to your child's life that you can ask relevant questions about their school, friends, and teachers. For example, "Did Sarah remember to hand in her project today? Last time she got into trouble for being late."

- Provide the opportunity for spontaneous conversation by having fun one-on-one time with your child. Take your child bowling or ask them to help you in the garden or garage, where a casual conversation might turn into something deep and revealing.

Provide Reassurance and Support

Listening to your children's challenges will make them feel validated and not alone in their struggles. Your children also need reassurance to help them see that most situations are temporary and that there are answers and support available.

However, when children constantly ask for repeated reassurance with questions such as "Are you really going to pick me up after school?" or "Are you sure that God hears my prayers?" it may be an indication of anxiety. Anxiety needs to be addressed at its root cause, and constant reassurance will only provide temporary comfort.

It can be hard to find the right words when your children need reassurance and comfort about a spiritual issue. Here are some ideas to help you say what they need to hear:

- "I can tell you are struggling with prayer recently, and I want to help if possible."

- "It is normal to have doubts. Tell me what bothers you, and we can discuss it. Perhaps we'll find an answer if we put our minds together."

- "I won't love you any less or have less respect for you if you struggle to have faith. I will support you and am always available if you need help or advice."

Embracing a Growth Mindset

It is important that our children understand that we can't have everything our way, that life isn't always fair, and that doubts and discouragement happen to everyone. Setbacks and challenges are opportunities for growth, even if it doesn't feel like it at the time. Part of our spiritual growth is to persevere in prayer and have faith when life gets hard.

A growth mindset in regard to faith is the belief that we can improve our relationship with God and be more faithful to His Word. We can only grow if we are willing to keep trying and keep our eyes on our goals. Here are some tips on how to cultivate a growth mindset:

- Consider doubts an opportunity to learn. For example, doubting whether Moses really parted the Red Sea may open an exciting world of research in archeology and geography. Doubting if prayers are answered offers the opportunity to interview family or community members and get to know them better while finding out if their prayer journey has been rewarding.

- To grow, you have to accept that sometimes you will fail. There will be times when your prayers aren't answered or when you make decisions that are contrary to God's will. Sincere prayers of forgiveness and a determination to do better next time will cleanse and nourish the spirit.

- Facing doubts, fears, setbacks, and challenges with courage, hope, and a growth mindset is the path to success and personal fulfillment. Add prayer to the mix and you can't go wrong!

Join me in the next chapter to explore the intersection between prayer and the community.

Chapter 11

PRAYER AND COMMUNITY INVOLVEMENT

In this chapter, we'll explore the role of a child's community in their prayer life and how a prayer community can enhance their spiritual growth and relationship with God.

Prayer Groups

Prayer groups can range from a single prayer buddy to an organized community prayer group. A prayer buddy is often a sibling or best friend who is available at times when the day needs a spiritual boost. Prayer groups are often organized by a local church and may include Bible study as well as prayer. These prayer groups have several benefits that can enrich children's prayer lives, which we'll explore in this section.

Community Support

Being part of a group where children feel they fit in can provide the encouragement and support they need to stick to their prayer routine and dedicate themselves to spiritual growth.

Having a set time for community prayer helps your children make prayer a routine. They learn how to be consistent, especially because the other group members will expect them to attend and hold them accountable if they neglect their prayers.

The prayer group is a place where children can share their burdens with believers who will pray with them, support them spiritually, and help them grow in faith.

Learning and Growing Together

One of the greatest gifts of prayer groups is witnessing how God works in the lives of others. We get to hear their prayers of gratitude when God shows His hand and learn to appreciate the challenges that foster spiritual resilience.

Our spiritual journey is one of learning. As we grow, we learn more about the nature of God, and our communication with Him deepens. A prayer group also enables us to learn more about others and how they communicate with God. These fresh perspectives can bring new prayer practices and open our minds to new ideas about worship.

Our faith grows when we join in the joy of a miracle or a prayer answered. As a community, we become united as servants of the same God, and our prayers extend beyond ourselves. Our prayers grow to focus on encouragement and intercession for group members as we become more spiritually aware of the needs of others and less self-centered.

People tend to gravitate toward others with the same interests and values. There is nothing like being part of a community of like-minded people to make someone feel that they do have a place in the world where they truly fit in and are part of a group that they can rely on.

The children who attend prayer groups share the same spiritual values as your child, which can be a relief for parents who are concerned about bad influences. Having friends with shared values will also help your children be proud and confident of their faith and prayer habits in a world where faith is often mocked.

It is a blessing to share in prayers with those who have unshakable, inspiring faith and to minister to others through our humble prayers. The people who live close to God can help guide your child toward a more spiritual outlook on life.

Social Skills

Joining a prayer group can do wonders for a child's ability to interact with adults and peers. Let's take a look at some ways a prayer group can improve and develop your child's social skills:

- Having an awareness of the needs of others contributes to the development of empathy, gratitude, and humility. In a prayer group, a child is confronted with the often unseen harsh realities faced by their friends and families. For example, your child might not have suspected that one of their classmates' families was struggling financially until hearing the friend pray for financial relief and blessings of food and rent money. Empathy will give your child the ability to truly connect with people sincerely and with consideration.

- A prayer community is a safe space without judgment where everyone has a sense of belonging while serving God together. This creates a solid safety net for the child who is still learning social interaction. The child gradually gains confidence in their ability to express themselves, and their verbal communication skills improve with every prayer.

- Your child may learn teamwork and cooperation skills if the prayer group includes activities such as outreach, organizing meals and visits for the sick and elderly, and neighborhood environmental cleanup projects.

- Taking turns praying or reading the Bible to the group lets your child's leadership skills blossom. They become aware that their words impact others and that they can use their words to help make the world a better place.

- Conflict can arise in even the most spiritually focused group. There may be a disagreement over the interpretation of scripture that becomes heated and ends with hurt feelings and frustration. Your child may have the opportunity to see how conflicts are handled constructively and learn the power of forgiveness.

How to Lead a Prayer Group for Children

If there aren't any prayer groups in your area that accept children, you may consider starting your own prayer group and inviting your children's friends and children from church to join in. Here are some tips to help your prayer group run smoothly:

- When the children pray out loud, limit everyone's prayer time to a maximum of two minutes. This limit gives everyone time to pray, is short enough for children with attention deficit issues to follow, and is long enough for a prayer of gratitude, repentance, or asking for blessings.

- Have extra Bibles available for children who didn't bring their own. Some children may find it easier to read a psalm or a special verse as a prayer. These prayers are also pleasing to God; after all, the Bible is His holy Word.

- Lighting a candle to symbolize prayer can add an atmosphere of reverence, but don't give young children candles or keep the lit candles where they can easily fall over or set something on fire. Children are adorable but not always responsible, and their little hands may be clumsy. Better safe than sorry!

- When the youngsters arrive, show them where they can sit and give them an enthusiastic welcome. Explain to the group that everyone will get a chance to pray and state the time limit. Large groups may necessitate shorter prayer times, such as a minute maximum per prayer.

- Explain that after your prayer, the turn to pray goes to the person to the right. Children who are too shy to pray out loud but who still want to be part of the group are welcome to either read a short passage from the Bible or pray silently. If a child prefers to pray silently, keep track of their prayer time, and after a minute or two has passed, the prayer passes to the next in line.

- Remind the group that prayer is sacred and that making fun of someone else's prayer or gossiping about what they pray about is insulting to God. Usually, children are very aware that prayer is special, and they will be very well behaved, but newcomers who have never attended a church or a prayer meeting before may not yet understand that prayer is holy.

- It will set the group at ease if you say the first prayer. Thank the Lord for everyone attending the group, and dedicate the group to His glory.

- After the last prayer, thank everyone for coming and set the date for the next meeting. If you have the time, space, and finances, let the children stay for cookies and soda. This will give the children the opportunity to get to know each other better and talk about spiritual matters.

Community Service and Prayer

God wants us to live our faith and be an example to others. A prayer group can include community service in its activities and goals, which will help your child develop compassion, gratitude, and selflessness.

Empathy Building

We've discussed how participating in a prayer group can help children develop empathy. Combine a prayer group with community service and your child's empathy and compassion may fine-tune into genuine selflessness and a desire to help others.

During church outreach and community service, children are exposed to lifestyles they haven't encountered before. Older children might get to see poverty, homelessness, debilitating illness, and isolation. These situations cause children to think twice about the challenges people face and make them aware of the blessings in their own lives.

It isn't necessary to expose your child to situations they would find too upsetting at their age. Community service can be as humble as donating coloring books to a hospital's children's wing or providing art supplies to a shelter.

The youth leader of the outreach or community service program can serve as a role model of compassion for children. Children can emulate the example of an adult who serves others from the heart because God inspired them to do so.

Practical Application

Children read in the Bible or hear testimonies of people who make a difference in others' lives and want to do the same. Prayer is the preparation, and community service is the action that can make a positive difference.

Remind your children that faith has an active component. Although prayer can move mountains, God enables us to take our own actions. The combination of prayer and action is the most effective way to change our society for the better.

If your child wants to partake in community service but doesn't know how or where to start, these tips may help:

- Donating their unwanted or outgrown clothes can be done directly to a family in need, a local thrift store, or a shelter. Another option is to visit the Giving Factory Direct website. Giving Factory Direct will match you with a child suffering from clothing insecurity and give you their shipping address (*Giving Factory Direct*, 2023).

- Giving food to your local food bank will help fill a needy person's belly. This can be extra food from your house, or older children may choose to buy the food with a part of their allowance.

- Tiny roadside free libraries encourage the neighborhood community to share their books. If there isn't one of these mailbox-sized libraries in your area, you can consider starting one with your children. You can find building plans on the Little Free Library website and register your little library if you wish (*Start Your Own Little Free Library*, n.d.). Your children will probably be enthusiastic in helping you start a neighborhood free toy library as well.

- Animals are part of the community too, and many shelters would be grateful to have more volunteers to help clean the kennels. Some shelters have programs available where children can read to the animals (great for the children's reading skills and calming for the animals) or play with them. Shelters will also appreciate donations of blankets, towels, pet food (for dogs, cats, and bunnies), bowls, toys, and cleaning products. Please make sure that you take your children to no-kill shelters. Kill shelters are traumatic for both the animals and the people who work there and are definitely not a place for children. However, the animals at kill shelters also have needs, and the shelter staff can pick up donations of food, blankets, towels, and bowls from your home.

- Many zoos or animal sanctuaries have programs where people can adopt an animal in exchange for a donation. The zoo or sanctuary gives a photo, a certificate, news, and regular updates about the adopted animal.

- Women who experience abuse and flee their homes seldom have time to pack more than the basic essentials, and many are unable to pack anything at all. A donation of personal products such as shampoo, deodorant, and unused makeup to a shelter or center for abuse victims can provide some basic necessities for women in crisis.

- A prayer group can show appreciation for the environment by forming a litter cleanup group on weekends. It is deeply satisfying to restore an area's natural beauty, and it gives children the opportunity to reflect on the glory of God's creation and the role of humanity in caring for it.

Cultivating Gratitude

Children who volunteer for community service or donate to a community program become aware that there are people and animals who get by with barely the basic essentials. Let's take a brief look at the impact of community service on a child's sense of gratitude:

- Being confronted with the effects of poverty, loneliness, illness, and abuse helps children understand that having a life with enough, and sometimes extra, resources is a privilege denied to many.

- Making a difference, even if it is small, teaches your children to be grateful for the positive role they can play in others' lives.

- Youth and community leaders who serve others in a spirit of gratitude and compassion can inspire your children to emulate them in both action and intention.

- Gratitude isn't only a blessing to the giver; it is also a gift from the receiver. Seeing how grateful a less privileged person can be for something basic and small helps a child realize how much they take for granted.

- Safety, security, health, and family are things we all tend to appreciate only when they are gone. Community service serves as a reminder to be grateful for all our blessings and to treasure what we have.

Learning Through Action

Being actively involved in community service can teach your child these valuable life skills:

- how to work in a team and coordinate efforts

- organizing and planning

- responsibility and accountability

- cultural awareness and social sensitivity

- efficient communication

- resilience

- empathy

- problem-solving and innovation

- building social networks

- being considerate of the needs of others

- appreciating and taking good care of possessions and resources

Participating in Religious Ceremonies

In this section, we'll briefly discuss the role religious ceremonies play in a child's spiritual journey. The ceremonies can range from rituals that the entire congregation can take part in, such as communion, to private events like baptism or family ceremonies, such as lighting a candle during prayer. The number of participants and the setting are irrelevant; a religious ceremony is any ritualized action with a spiritual meaning.

Cultural Connection

Religious ceremonies provides children with rituals rooted in culture and tradition. Children learn about the historical figures or events portrayed by the ceremonies and discover the meanings behind traditional practices. This knowledge transforms an ordinary prayer during a ceremony into a connection with history and spiritual figures such as saints and martyrs.

The cultural connection can include mantras, chants, liturgies, and hymns in unfamiliar languages. An example of this is the Latin hymn *Ave Maria*, which connects the modern with the ancient through the traditional language of the early church. While children don't have to learn Latin to pray or sing in church, they can appreciate the angelic message behind the hymn and get a sense of the ancient, unbroken tradition of their faith.

Family ceremonies connect a child with the mini-culture of their relatives. Every family has tales, habits, and histories particular to them, and being a part of this gives children the emotional safety net of kinfolk. If the ceremonies are religious, they also add similar values and shared faith to their family's cultural connection.

Symbolic Meanings

Every traditional belief system has symbols particular to it, and understanding their deeper meaning can give children a sense of context and connection to the origins of their faith. For example, the dove is a symbol of the outpouring of the Holy Spirit, and when children understand the deeper reality behind the image, their prayers and reflections on the Holy Spirit are deepened.

Symbols can include images, statues, and objects such as the cross. Each symbol has a story to tell, and exploring these stories can ignite a passion for the history and traditions of faith.

Community Bonding

Taking part in a religious ceremony, such as communion, makes a child realize that they are part of the body of Christ and bonded with other believers through faith. This contributes to the selflessness that is the foundation of service to others and genuine compassion.

Religious festivals are an opportunity for a community to come together and bond in celebration over shared traditions. For example, Christmas allows Christians all over the world to share the spirit of goodwill and celebrate the birth of Jesus with fellow believers. Above all, religious celebrations bring an element of fun into our spiritual journey.

Spiritual Reflection

Some ceremonies and traditions are based on events revered for their moral lessons. When children partake in these ceremonies, it reinforces the moral values and causes them to reflect on their own spirituality and the role of morality in their everyday lives.

During a ceremony, such as communion, children can connect with God through an act that makes the divine tangible. The abstract concept of divine sacrifice is made concrete through the ritualistic re-enactment of the wine and bread of the Last Supper. By eating the wafer and drinking the wine, the child gets to partake in a tradition that is almost 2,000 years old and still spiritually poignant today.

Connecting With Other Families Who Pray

If you pray as a family, have you ever wondered if other families also have prayer time? The earliest churches consisted of families meeting for prayer and scripture reading, sometimes with a short homily or testimony from a member who felt moved by the Holy Spirit to speak. Let's explore the value of connecting with other praying families in modern times.

Shared Values

Deep, lasting friendships are built on commonalities. Families who befriend others with the same values know they have something very important in common and can encourage and counsel each other in ways that stay true to their beliefs.

Friends who have the same moral and ethical values can be a source of emotional support and encourage you to stay faithful in your spiritual dedication, especially when circumstances tempt you to give up.

Peer Influence

Befriending other believing families provides your children with more role models they can emulate. There comes a natural phase in children's lives when they question and criticize many things their parents do. Having other adults who they can trust will give them someone to turn to when they don't want to ask their parents.

If the other family has children around the same age as yours, the children can be good influences on each other. It will be easier for your children to resist negative peer pressure when they have friends with the same outlook and values.

You'll have more peace of mind when your children are doing a community service project with a praying peer than spending time with so-called friends who want to convince your child to experiment with sex, drugs, alcohol, and Satanism. Unfortunately, many children without strong values and spiritual roots may feel unsure about themselves and more inclined to engage in unhealthy activities when they have others joining them.

Shared Activities

It is simply more fun to share religious celebrations and prayer requests with like-minded people. Befriending other believing families adds to the joy of sharing our traditions and festivals with those who appreciate their value and meaning.

There is a wide variety of activities praying families can enjoy together, such as:

- prayer meetings

- Easter egg painting

- Easter egg hunts

- Christmas caroling

- Christmas dinner

- Thanksgiving dinner

- visits to museums, parks, historical battlegrounds, or other places of interest

- community service projects

- taking turns babysitting and picking the kids up from school

Learning Opportunities

Anything we do regularly can become a stale habit, and prayer is no exception! Even with the best of intentions, we might end up stuck in a rut where we repeat the same prayers and read the same verses. There's nothing wrong with a pair of old, comfortable shoes, but we outgrow them and need a new pair now and again. The same goes for prayer; we have our familiar favorites, but refreshing our prayer life can rekindle the sparkle in our spirit.

Connecting with other praying families exposes us to fresh perspectives and new ideas that we can incorporate into our own prayer practices. We might also be inspired by their traditions and bring something new into our family prayer time that everyone enjoys.

In the next chapter, we will look at the prayer journey itself, focusing on milestones, future goals, success stories, and planning for the future.

Chapter 12

CELEBRATING PRAYER ACHIEVEMENTS

In this final chapter, we recognize and celebrate the prayer journey and look ahead to the future. Let's start with the milestones on your child's prayer journey.

Milestone Celebrations

In a previous chapter, we explored how to set achievable, realistic goals. When your child achieves a milestone, such as achieving a goal, completing a year of community service, or starting a prayer group, a celebration is a great way to acknowledge their efforts. It also offers the family or faith community an opportunity to find encouragement, hope, and inspiration from the positive outcome.

Reflecting on Progress

Starting a prayer habit involves careful goal setting and planning. Sticking to a prayer routine requires self-discipline and a lot of faith. Those are the qualities worth celebrating. Sometimes we don't realize how far we've come until we look back at how we started and progressed on our journey. When your children reflect on how much their prayer life has evolved, they will be motivated to set new, bigger goals and grow even more spiritually.

What Are Prayer Milestones?

Prayer milestones are markers that indicate we've accomplished something specific that will help us reach our goals. Children's milestones should take their age into account; it is unreasonable to expect a five-year-old to memorize the *Lord's Prayer*, but their first turn saying grace at dinner would be an appropriate milestone.

Here are a few prayer milestones that are worthy of celebrating:

- Teaching a very young child to pray usually happens with the child repeating words after the parent. The child's first prayer on their own is worthy of a celebration. Make note of the date, and write this and other prayer milestones in a journal to give your child as a gift on their 16th birthday. They'll be delighted to see how much they've grown!

- The first time your child can fluently recite a prayer central to your faith, such as the *Lord's Prayer* or the

Hail Mary, is a significant milestone. It signifies that your child has taken their first steps in following an age-old faith tradition and becoming part of that community.

- Once your child has consistently formed a habit of praying in the morning, at mealtime, and at bedtime, it's time for a small celebration. (It takes about a month for the habit to fully take hold.)

- The milestones involving religious ceremonies depend on your faith tradition and denomination and can include baptism, the first communion, first Sunday school or catechism classes, a bar or bat mitzvah, or being old enough to attend a youth service.

- Very young children find it hard to fully understand their own needs and can't really comprehend the needs of others. Once you've noticed that your child has grown enough to be concerned about others, you can let them join in the prayer requests. But keep it age-appropriate. Your child may join in prayer for a sick uncle or a sibling who has upcoming exams, but it would be very inappropriate to allow them to join a prayer session about adult concerns such as abuse, financial insecurity, or terminal illness. The first time your child can take part in your family's prayer requests deserves a milestone celebration, even if it is only something small, such as praying that Aunt Mary's parrot regrows its feathers.

Involving Family and Friends

A milestone is a big deal to the person achieving it, and it is disappointing and disheartening if no one else notices or cares about the goal reached or the first steps taken. It isn't always possible to involve other people in a celebration, but a short congratulatory phone call or a handshake can mean the world to a small child who naturally craves approval and praise.

Here are some ways you can have a larger celebration for special milestones and involve family and friends:

- A small cookies and soda celebration at home with special prayers of thanks and blessing is more than enough to form a lasting, warm memory and acknowledge the importance of your child's milestone.

- You can involve your church community when a big milestone is achieved, such as an extraordinary academic or sports achievement, or if God answers a prayer in a miraculous way. Ask your priest, pastor, or youth leader to say a special prayer of thanksgiving to testify to the grace of God's blessings.

- Family history should be kept alive and vibrant, and one of the ways to accomplish this is to have older family members share their experiences. Deepen family bonds and make your children aware of the role of God in your family's history by having a story evening. During this gathering, other family members and friends can share their experiences of the milestone your child achieved. Perhaps you can make a video where your child and older family members talk about their first communion, baptism, or any other milestone and show photos of the event.

- If you have access to a garden, you may consider planting a tree in celebration. If not, a new low-maintenance houseplant can also symbolize your child's spiritual growth, and your child can tend to the plant.

- Be inventive and start a family blessing ceremony where each family member and invited friends can gift your child a little written prayer or Bible verse. These prayers can be kept in a prayer journal and become a sentimental keepsake to be passed down to your grandchildren one day.

Setting Future Goals

Once a goal has been achieved and the celebrations are done, the next step is to set bigger goals with an eye on future growth. Here are some ideas to help your child use prayer milestones as stepping stones for their spiritual future:

- When looking back at what has been achieved, discuss with your child what they have learned from the experience. What would they do the same or differently if they could travel back in time? Did your child learn anything regarding goal setting that might be useful in their everyday lives?

- Encourage your child to set bigger prayer goals. For example, if your child's goal is to learn the *Lord's Prayer*, suggest they try memorizing a Bible chapter.

The goals must become more complex and challenging; otherwise, the result isn't growth and achievement but complacency and stasis.

- Keep expanding prayer experience by exploring new things. Your children can research how other denominations or faiths approach prayer and discuss how those methods fit or clash with their personal experience of prayer.

- Future goals involving prayer should include prayer in action, such as community service, prayer requests, worship services, and participating in outreach programs.

- Emphasize that goal setting is a lifetime commitment. Every goal reached demands a new and bigger prize to aim for.

Sharing Success Stories

We all love a happy ending and get inspired when we hear how someone overcame their challenges to meet their goals. In this section, we'll explore how sharing our spiritual successes can affect the people around us.

Inspiration and Encouragement

Testimonies of spiritual successes inspire us to work on our own spirituality and to persevere, have faith, and keep trying no matter what. There are many ways in which success stories affect us:

- When we hear about the spiritual struggles of others, we realize we're not alone in the challenges we face. A success story shows us that there is a way out, and we are reassured that we are like iron purified by fire; it hurts to get burned by the fires of hardship, but our trials and tribulations make us stronger and spiritually resilient.

- Testimonies validate our faith by letting us know that God really answers prayers, performs miracles, and is involved in our lives. They serve as proof that faith isn't a fantasy built on a fairytale but has concrete, real-world effects.

- Telling our own success stories allows us to reflect on the role prayer and faith have played in our plans and achievements. We notice how our outlooks have changed and how we've matured. Knowing how and why we have changed is part of the wisdom of knowing oneself. Introspection allows us to identify the parts of ourselves we need to work on and fosters gratitude for the person we have become.

- If you've been neglecting your spirituality, listening to testimonies can stir your spirit back into action. Becoming aware of how God rewards dedication and faith can bring us back into the prayer closet.

Building a Support Network

A support network of other believers provides a safety net to help us avoid falling into apostasy, spiritual laziness, and dark doubts. Sharing our successes, failures, and need for guidance builds a community that is open and honest, where everyone can feel safe to share in a nonjudgmental space. This is how sharing your stories can build a solid and supportive community network:

- Being honest about your spirituality fosters an authentic environment where no one has to hide their failures or doubts. Sharing success stories should be about the power and grace of God, not a competition where people feel pressured to hide their struggles to win acceptance from the group.

- A support network of like-minded believers who are sensitive and compassionate about everyone's challenges is a shield against loneliness, depression, and despondency. All it takes to build such a supportive community is the willingness to be emotionally vulnerable and share what is in your heart.

- Sharing both the ups and downs and accepting dialogue about your challenges exposes you to possible solutions, fresh points of view, and helpful insights.

Celebrating Collective Achievements

We've discussed the importance of celebrating your children's achievements and revisiting your family's spiritual milestones, but what about collective achievements? Prayer groups, youth groups, community service groups, and the congregation all have their own goals and milestones that should be recognized and celebrated to foster camaraderie, appreciation, and gratitude.

Here are some examples of collective spiritual achievements and how they might be celebrated:

- A prayer group may occasionally have periods of fasting, which can be celebrated with a communal meal.

- If the entire congregation achieves a goal, such as fund-raising a certain amount or completing a prayer chain, it can be acknowledged with a prayer breakfast, a special service to give thanks, or, if there are musicians in the congregation, a new hymn composed to celebrate the community's shared efforts.

- When the group reaches the goal of a certain number of members, buying or renting an ideal meeting space, or renovating their current space, the hard work can be rewarded with a celebration such as a group picnic or barbecue. Be sensitive toward those without the finances to pay for their own food at these get-togethers and have extra corn on the cob and freshly baked bread available for everyone so that hungry members who can't afford picnic or barbecue food can eat from the communal table without embarrassment. A new or renovated venue can also be celebrated by having a dance party or a play by the local amateur theatre group.

- Some prayer groups aim to read through the entire Bible and cover one chapter a day. Reading through all the books is a remarkable achievement and can be celebrated with a festival, cake and coffee meeting, or perhaps inviting a Bible scholar to give a talk.

- Alerting local newspapers or TV channels is a good way to inspire the community while giving acknowledgment and thanks to everyone who contributed toward the goal.

- Awards such as certificates or trophies that can be displayed are excellent motivators for the future and serve as recognition of a job well done. Trophies don't cost an arm and a leg, and anyone with a printer and quality paper can create certificates of achievement for the group.

Evaluating the Journey So Far

In this section, we'll look at ways to track and assess your children's spiritual development and the impact prayer has on their lives.

Assessing Growth and Development

When evaluating the impact of prayer on our children and observing how their spirits are developing and maturing, we can examine their behavior to measure their progress. Your children should also engage in self-assessment to become aware of their growth and see how God remains active in their lives.

It isn't always easy to see gradual differences in people we see every day. We expect our children to develop in every way, so it can be hard to determine what effects prayer has had on them. The following tips can help you track their spiritual development:

- Keep an eye out for behavioral changes that signify blossoming emotional maturity, such as improved patience and a calmer, more controlled response to stress.

- Your child's attitude can be greatly affected by prayer. Diligent prayer and an awareness of spiritual values can lead to a more optimistic, grateful, and helpful attitude.

- Observe your children's interaction with others and how they talk about them. Prayer that goes beyond self-focus develops understanding and empathy toward others.

- Sticking to a prayer routine develops a sense of responsibility and duty.

- Prayer fosters an understanding of the importance of forgiveness. A praying child might be more inclined to accept the flaws of others and not get upset over small matters.

Identifying Areas for Improvement

Identify areas where your children can improve, not for the purpose of criticizing or chastising them, but to encourage them with praise and support. Have compassion for your children's faults and be mindful that they aren't yet fully developed people.

Here are some ways you can identify and help remedy weaker areas in your children's spiritual development:

- Find out how well your children understand the abstract concepts of your faith with open-ended questions such as "What do you think the Holy Spirit is?" The answers will show you areas where your children may need more guidance.

- Your children's ability to regulate their emotions, such as frustration, annoyance, disappointment, anger, and impatience, increases as they mature spiritually. If your children have difficulty with these emotions, spending more time in prayer and self-reflection may help them cope better. Be aware that sometimes problems with emotional regulation don't have a spiritual basis. Your child may be the victim of bullying or abuse or have a physical or psychological issue. Speak to a children's health professional if regular prayer has no effect on their emotional development.

- If your children aren't sticking to their prayer routine, they might need help developing self-discipline. It could also be that prayer time is boring for them, which is nothing to be concerned about. Make prayer time more engaging for the youngsters by incorporating visual aids like posters, sharing stories, using colorful illustrated Bibles, and taking them for prayer walks.

Planning for Continued Spiritual Growth

Our spirits never stop growing as long as we feed ourselves a steady diet of prayer, faith, scripture, worship, praise, and self-reflection. In the final section of this book, we'll take a quick look at how you can help your children plan for continued spiritual growth.

Setting Long-Term Goals

Focus on the future with long-term goals that will result in a closer relationship with God, such as the following:

Be consistent with a prayer routine. Make it a long-term goal to pray daily for a year. When that is achieved, extend it to 10 years, and after that, pray every day for the rest of your life.

When life hits you with doubts or low points, be determined to persist in prayer. Have a goal to keep praying even if you don't feel like it.

A long-term goal of reading a passage from the Bible daily until you've read every verse will enhance your faith. But don't merely read the words; reflect on how the passage relates to your life and your spiritual journey.

Long-term goals can involve your community. Your goal may include others, such as spending an additional hour per week on community service, fundraising for a specific project, or attending every meeting of a prayer group for the next year.

Adapting Practices

Imagine you set a goal to run a mile by a certain date. If you keep to your training schedule, you'll achieve your goal fairly easily. But now that you can run a mile, you need something bigger to aim for, such as a five-mile fun run. The techniques learned in achieving your previous goal can be used to prepare for your fun run, and you'll also have insight into what training methods don't work for you.

Spiritual goals work the same way. Your children will learn when and how to pray more effectively and adjust their prayer routines accordingly. Encourage them to be flexible when they have to be without slacking off and to use what they have learned to avoid unnecessary obstacles.

Seeking Guidance and Finding Resources

There may be times when your children need a little extra encouragement on their spiritual journey. Here are some external resources your child might benefit from:

- Sunday school, usually offered by your local church

- church or community mission projects for community service and outreach

- community- or church-based mentorship programs

- summer camps that feature Bible study, prayer, and worship

- faith-based youth groups and clubs

- Bible study apps and prayer apps

Now that you have come to the end of this chapter, consider yourself a prayer expert and be inspired to lead your children on their spiritual journey. Join me in the conclusion, where we will have a recap of the key points discussed in this book.

CONCLUSION

We've discussed the importance of prayer and how to teach young children to talk to God. You've found ideas on how to make prayer more engaging to young minds and how to answer the difficult questions regarding the unfairness of life, the nature of God, and the afterlife. We've examined different prayer traditions and learned about the spiritual value of community service. Hopefully, this book has provided you not only with ideas on how to encourage your children to pray but also with ways to enrich your own prayer habits.

You now have all the tools, tips, and strategies to lead your children toward a fulfilling prayer life and a deep relationship with their Creator. Prayer should be as natural and comfortable as breathing. With gentle encouragement, fun activities, support from their family and friends, and age-appropriate goals, your children will soon cultivate a prayer habit that will last a lifetime. It is very likely that they will one day teach their own children how to pray with the same methods you are using and share fond memories of their own journey with their grandkids. Prayer can be part of your family tradition for many generations to come. A personal relationship with God is a beautiful legacy that will inspire many.

Remember to encourage your children to keep developing their spirituality and relationship with God. Prayer needs to be regular and consistent, not just an emergency appeal for help. They should be aware that God is everywhere, all the time, and they should understand that God wants to be a part of their lives always in everything they do. Recognize and celebrate their milestones and reward their accomplishments, even if it means simply letting them skip chores for a day. Children thrive on approval and praise, and acknowledging their hard work will give them the incentive to try even harder and aim for ever greater goals in the future. Help them set realistic, achievable goals and, where possible, assist them in reaching these goals without taking over.

Don't underestimate the role of the community in your children's development. Prayer extends beyond the prayer closet, so let your children experience the power of praying with others. By being active members of a community, such as a prayer group or community service organization, children can see faith in action and prayers answered. The possibilities of connecting your children's faith with people beyond your immediate family are endless, and you can easily start your own community project.

Above all, the best teaching method is to set an example. Your children need to see you pray consistently and sincerely through both good times and bad. Aim to live in such a way that makes your children want to emulate you. Be an example of patience, compassion, faith, honesty, kindness, and resilience. Some children might rebel against their parents when they are teens, but that stage passes quickly, and then they come to appreciate and seek out the traditions and guidance of their elders, so be patient with your young ones. Step up and be the person you want your children to become.

Encourage your children to keep exploring prayer and discovering fresh ideas. They can be flexible and adapt their traditions to suit their individual preferences and spiritual needs. They might benefit from experimenting with various prayer styles, such as using a prayer wheel, prayer beads, or a prayer shawl. Warn your children to keep their prayer life active and engaging. A stale prayer life is not conducive to spiritual growth. Just like a plant can't grow without water, the spirit can't thrive without sincere, regular prayer. Remind your children that prayer is a good, healthy habit that is as important to the spirit as a healthy diet is to the body.

The ultimate goal of teaching your children how to pray is to help them develop an unshakable faith and a character pleasing to God. By laying a strong foundation for your children's spiritual growth, you give them a gift that will last an eternity. Their relationship with our loving Father will be a source of comfort, joy, and inspiration in this life and a shining light in Heaven forever.

Here's a list of notable mentions of children in the Bible:

Matthew 19:14 - "Let the little children come to me, and do not hinder them, for the kingdom of heaven belongs to such as these."

Psalm 127:3 - "Children are a heritage from the Lord, offspring a reward from him."

Proverbs 22:6 - "Train up a child in the way he should go; even when he is old he will not depart from it."

Mark 10:13-16 - Jesus blessing the little children

Deuteronomy 6:7 - Instructions to teach children God's commandments

1 Samuel 3:1-21 - Young Samuel hearing God's voice

2 Kings 5:2-3 - The young servant girl who told Naaman about Elisha

Daniel 1:3-17 - Daniel and his young friends in Babylon

Luke 2:41-52 - Jesus as a 12-year-old in the temple

2 Timothy 3:15 - Timothy learning scripture from childhood

Exodus 2:1-10 - Baby Moses in the basket

1 Samuel 16:11-13 - Young David being anointed king

Matthew 18:3 - "Unless you become like little children…"

Ephesians 6:1-4 - Instructions for children to obey parents

Colossians 3:20 - Children obeying parents in everything

REFERENCES

Anderson, J. W., & Nunnelley, P. A. (2016). Private prayer associations with depression, anxiety and other health conditions: an analytical review of clinical studies. *Postgraduate Medicine, 128*(7), 635–641. https://doi.org/10.1080/00325481.2016.1209962

The benefits of being in a prayer group. (2021, September 28). Val Marie Paper. https://www.valmariepaper.com/the-benefits-praying-prayer-group/

Bernstein, J. (2023, February 19). *5 supportive things to say when your child is sad.* Psychology Today. https://www.psychologytoday.com/us/blog/liking-the-child-you-love/202302/5-supportive-things-to-say-when-your-child-is-sad

Birch, J. (n.d.). *Prayers on a theme of Thanksgiving.* Faith & worship. https://www.faithandworship.com/prayers_Thanksgiving

Blessing. A. G. (2024, July 25). *Showing gratitude through community service with Mother Mary.* Angel Grace Blessing. https://angelgraceblessing.com/showing-gratitude-through-community-service-with-mother-mary/

Chen, Y., & VanderWeele, T. J. (2018). Associations of religious upbringing with subsequent health and well-being from adolescence to young adulthood: An outcome-wide analysis. *American Journal of Epidemiology, 187*(11), 2355–2364. https://doi.org/10.1093/aje/kwy142

Children's doubts about God. (2024, January 29). Focus on the Family. https://www.focusonthefamily.com/family-qa/childrens-doubts-about-god/

Crain, N. (2012, January 19). *What to teach kids about unanswered prayer.* Natasha Crain. https://natashacrain.com/what-to-teach-kids-about-unanswered-prayer/

Creating a prayer space with your kids. (n.d.). Raising Prayerful Kids. https://www.raisingprayerfulkids.com/blog/creating-a-prayer-space-with-your-kids

Davis, T. (2024, May 29). *15 ways to build a growth mindset.* Psychology Today. https://www.psychologytoday.com/us/blog/click-here-for-happiness/201904/15-ways-to-build-a-growth-mindset

Dean. (2020, October 28). *25 Christian prayer methods you can implement.* Just Disciple. https://justdisciple.com/prayer-method/

Edifa. (2021, January 26). *Can children be taught to pray silently?* Aleteia. https://aleteia.org/cp1/2021/01/26/can-children-be-taught-to-pray-silently

Editor in Chief. (2019, November 1). *20 most famous prayers of all-time.* ConnectUS. https://connectusfund.org/20-most-famous-prayers-of-all-time

Five ways God answers prayer. (n.d.). Christianity Today. https://store.christianitytoday.com/blogs/articles/five-ways-god-answers-prayer

Freire, K. (2021, November 1). *Christian prayer bracelets: Significance and uses.* Just Disciple. https://justdisciple.com/christian-prayer-bracelets/

Gaines, G. (2023a, December 4). *Exploring Christian prayer traditions: A comprehensive guide.* Jesus Prayer Ministry.com. https://jesusprayerministry.com/christian-prayer-traditions/

Gaines, G. (2023b, December 18). *Finding strength: Resilience through prayer (Biblical)*. Youthandreligion.com. https://youthandreligion.com/resilience-through-prayer-biblical/

Gaines, G. (2023c, December 21). *Exploring Christian prayer traditions & rituals*. Jesus Prayer Ministry.com. https://jesusprayerministry.com/christian-prayer-traditions-2/

Giving Factory Direct. (2023, August 28). Cradles to Crayons. https://www.cradlestocrayons.org/givingfactorydirect/

Gordon, S. (2021, September 20). *Why developing critical thinking skills is important*. Verywell Family. https://www.verywellfamily.com/how-to-teach-your-child-to-be-a-critical-thinker-5190765

Hopler, W. (2023, April 17). *Why do Catholics pray the rosary and what does it mean?* Crosswalk.com. https://www.crosswalk.com/faith/prayer/why-do-catholics-pray-the-rosary.html

How to create your very own prayer journal. (2020, February 14). Rooted + Grounded. https://rootedandgrounded.com/blogs/news/prayer-journal

How to teach young children about prayer. (2024, February 5). The Daily Grace Co. https://thedailygraceco.com/blogs/the-daily-grace-blog/how-to-teach-young-children-about-prayer

"I didn't make it!" How to help your child with disappointment. (2017, March 10). *Blogs.bible.org*. https://blogs.bible.org/i-didnt-make-it-how-to-help-your-child-with-disappointment/

Jans-Beken, L., Jacobs, N., Janssens, M., Peeters, S., Reijnders, J., Lechner, L., & Lataster, J. (2019). Gratitude and health: An updated review. *The Journal of Positive Psychology, 15*(6), 1–40. https://doi.org/10.1080/174 39760.2019.1651888

Joe. (2022, February 27). *11 emotional benefits of playdough.* Early Impact Learning. https://earlyimpactlearning. com/11-emotional-benefits-of-playdough/

Kauflin, B. (2023, September 21). *The physicality of faithful worship: Why we bend knees and lift hands.* Desiring God. https://www.desiringgod.org/articles/the-physi-cality-of-faithful-worship

Keeling, S. (2020, April 22). *A kids' prayer closet in 6 easy steps.* Sarah Keeling. https://www.sarah-keeling.com/post/a-kids-prayer-closet-in-6-easy-steps

Kropf, J. (2024, July 16). *115 easy rewards for kids (motivation without the candy).* Healthy Happy Impactful. https://healthyhappyimpactful.com/rewards-for-kids-ideas/

Lindenberger, B. (2024, August 21). *Goal setting for kids: Empowering future achievers to reach limitless Goals.* SUCCESS. https://www.success.com/goal-setting-for-kids/

Long, L. (2021, July 6). *Lord's Prayer craft idea: A colorful bracelet for kids.* ChurchLeaders. https://churchlead-ers.com/children/400333-lords-prayer-craft-bracelet. html

Matthew 18:20 for where two or three gather together in My name, there am I with them. "(n.d.). Bible Hub. https://biblehub.com/matthew/18-20.htm

McCready, A. (2024, April 16). *Helping kids open up: 7 tips to improve communication.* Positive Parenting Solutions. https://www.positiveparentingsolutions.com/parenting/help-kids-open-up-improve-communication

My Jewish Learning. *Kippah, tallit and tefillin.* (n.d.). My Jewish Learning. https://www.myjewishlearning.com/article/kippah-tallit-and-tefilin-the-clothing-of-jewish-prayer/

Patrick, M. (2012, August 2). *Leading a prayer meeting for kids.* Ministry-To-Children. https://ministry-to-children.com/leading-a-prayer-meeting-for-kids/

Pelini, S. (2018, January 17). *An age-by-age guide to helping kids manage emotions.* The Gottman Institute. https://www.gottman.com/blog/age-age-guide-helping-kids-manage-emotions/

Rice, D. W. (2018, January 31). *Seeking too much: Why constantly reassuring your children isn't always good.* Rice Psychology Group. https://ricepsychology.com/blog/parenting/seeking-too-much-why-constantly-reassuring-your-children-isnt-always-good/

Samples, K. (2006, October 1). *Faith and reason.* Reasons to Believe. https://reasons.org/explore/publications/connections/faith-and-reason

Samuel, S. (2023, September 4). *15 prayers in the Old Testament (Bible verse included).* PrayerSaves. https://www.prayersaves.com/prayers-in-the-old-testament/

Scientist. (n.d.). *25 famous scientists who believed in God.* Famous Scientists. https://www.famousscientists.org/25-famous-scientists-who-believed-in-god/

SoulfulPrayers. (2023, October 13). *Prayer in different religions: A comparative analysis.* Prayer Warriors. https://prayer-warriors.com/prayer-different-religions-comparative-analysis/

Spontaneous prayers. (2024, July 6). Kids Corner. https://kidscorner.net/devotions/spontaneous-prayers

Start your own little free library. (n.d.). Little Free Library. https://littlefreelibrary.org/start/

Tony. (2024, April 11). *38 community service projects for kids of all ages*. Kid Activities. https://kidactivities.net/community-service-ideas-for-kids-all-ages/

Traditional Catholic prayers. (n.d.). Scripture Catholic. https://www.scripturecatholic.com/traditional-catholic-prayers/

Trehub, S. E., Ghazban, N., & Corbeil, M. (2015). Musical affect regulation in infancy. *Annals of the New York Academy of Sciences, 1337*(1), 186–192. https://doi.org/10.1111/nyas.12622

Tucker, P. R. (2023, December 4). *Comparing prayer practices across religions*. Maxkol. https://www.maxkol.org/prayer-in-different-religions/

Uclahealth. (2021, November 10). *A guide to toxic stress in kids*. UCLA Health. https://www.uclahealth.org/news/article/a-guide-to-toxic-stress-in-kids

Vann, M. R., & Garone, S. (2023, October 5). *How prayer strengthens your emotional health*. Everyday Health. https://www.everydayhealth.com/emotional-health/power-of-prayer.aspx

Weir, M. (2022, January 5). *15+ powerful tips for silent prayer: The ultimate guide*. Pray with Confidence. https://praywithconfidence.com/silent-prayer/

Wendling, J. (n.d.). *6 ways to build a strong family prayer routine*. Family Christian. https://www.familychristian.com/family-life/6-ways-to-build-a-strong-family-prayer-routine/

The wheels on the bus. (n.d.). Super Simple. https://super-simple.com/song/wheels-on-the-bus/

Williams, A. (2024, January 14). *How to teach children about God: A comprehensive guide for parents.* Christian Website. https://www.christianwebsite.com/how-to-teach-children-about-god/

Williamson, T. (2021, June 1). *10 breathing exercises for kids with anxiety or anger.* Mindfulmazing. https://www.mindfulmazing.com/10-breathing-exercises-for-kids-with-anxiety-or-anger/